Historic
Ellicott City

A Walking Tour

D1503093

Joetta Cramm

Edited by Healan Barrow

A Greenberg Tours of America Publication

Published by

Greenberg Publishing Company, Inc.
7566 Main Street
Sykesville, MD 21784
(301) 795-7447

Manufactured in the United States of America

First Edition

Greenberg Publishing Company, Inc. offers the world's largest selection of Lionel, American Flyer and other toy train publications as well as a selection of books on other collectibles such as toys, marbles, and dollhouses. This publication is part of Greenberg's Tours of America series. For a copy of our current catalogue, send a stamped, self-addressed large envelope to Greenberg Publishing Company, Inc. at the above address.

ISBN 0-89778-154-6

Library of Congress Cataloging-in-Publication Data
Cramm, Joetta M., 1932-
    Historical Ellicott City : a walking tour / by Joetta M. Cramm; edited by Healan Barrow. - - 1st ed.
        p.   cm.

    ISBN 0-89778-154-6 : $7.9
    1. Ellicott City (Md) -- Description -- Tours.   2. Walking -- Maryland -- Ellicott City -- Guide-books   3. Historic sites -- Maryland -- Ellicott City   I. Barrow, Healan.   II. Title.
F189.E4C73   1990
917.52'81 -- dc20   90-35473
                                                                                                             CIP

Cover painting and design by Maureen Crum.

Table of Contents

PREFACE

Welcome to Ellicott City. Throughout these pages you will meet the people who made the town what it is today.

Change, as you will see, is constant and has given the town great vitality. As buildings undergo renovation, earlier construction methods have been uncovered. Contractors today are amazed at the sturdy building methods and materials used 150 to 200 years ago. Even today, Ellicott City is constantly changing. The businesses listed at the various addresses throughout this book are current as of May, 1990. No doubt some of these will change in the years to come; however I name them here to maintain a record for the future.

Many people, several of whom have spent most of their lives in Ellicott City, contributed to this book; without their support, it would not have been written. My appreciation and thanks to **Russell Moxley**, the former police chief; **B. Harrison Shipley, Jr.; Helen** and the late **Tracy Stackhouse; Anita Cushing; Mary Ann Marino; Dr. Irving Taylor; Julius Kinlein; Bladen Yates**; and the many others who helped with interviews and comments. **Mary Mannix**, librarian at the Howard County Historical Society, and many Society volunteers provided generous assistance. Photographs came from many sources, including **B. Harrison Shipley, Jr., John Kirkwood, Allan Hafner, John Slack, Cora Higinbothom, Bill Larricos, Shirley Peach**, the **Commercial and Farmers Bank**, the **Howard County Historical Society**, the **Peale Museum**, and the **Maryland Historical Society**. **Leigh Wachter** was especially helpful with his photographic expertise.

My special thanks to **Healan Barrow** who edited the manuscript and to **Linda Greenberg** who urged me to write a walking guide to Ellicott City. Finally, my thanks to the many people at the Greenberg Publishing Company who collaborated with me: **Samuel Baum** very capably supervised the book's overall production; **Terri Glaser** edited and prepared the book for publication; and **Cyndie Bare** and **Donna Price** proofread the many galleys. **Maureen Crum**, staff artist, designed both the cover and the title page, and created the watercolor painting for the cover.

Joetta Cramm
May 1990

Introduction

In 1850 Ellicotts Mills was a growing, bustling community. In the foreground is Baltimore County with early mills and homes. In the distance is Anne Arundel County (Howard County today) with its courthouse, schools, churches, dwellings, and businesses. During this time there was discussion of renaming Ellicotts Mills "Patapsco."

"It is just a small settlement, a shallow river beside which looms a group of tall mills and spanned by a graceful concrete bridge. Over this he [the motorist] rushes into and up a narrow, hilly main street upon which houses new and old, high and squatty, fresh painted and prosperous, elbow each other for room; and so past all this, into the open country again and the place is forgotten.

"Forgotten because unknown. He has passed through... If he would know her [Ellicott City] he must go to her reverently on foot. She will not reveal herself to the hasty and the superficial, because haste and superficiality have had no part in the fashioning of her."

This was the special charm of Ellicott City, as described in 1926 by Grace H. Sherwood, a writer with the *Baltimore Sun*. Written many years ago, her

words still capture the physical presence of the town. Today, the old buildings provide the town's thread of continuity.

To really know Ellicott City, we still must approach "reverently on foot."

SETTLEMENT AT ELLICOTTS MILLS — 1771

Joseph, Andrew, and John Ellicott were Quakers who had grown up in
Bucks County, Pennsylvania, the sons of Andrew Ellicott, an Englishman
who came to the Pennsylvania colony in 1730. Andrew married, had five
sons, and died young, leaving his widow to raise the young family. As the
boys grew they were apprenticed to learn the trades that led to their later
success in Maryland.

Lush vegetation and the swiftly flowing Patapsco River must have
captivated the three Ellicott brothers when they searched for land in the late
1760s. The brothers had searched throughout Maryland and Pennsylvania
for a site where they could grow wheat and harness water power for a mill.
In 1771 the Ellicott brothers purchased many acres east of the river in the
valley known as the "Hollow." Although the valley was uninhabited, they
were not alone; other settlers lived along the bluffs overlooking the river.

Some of the tracts of land the Ellicotts bought later spanned both sides of
the Patapsco; the west bank was part of Anne Arundel County (now Howard
County), and the east bank was in Baltimore County.

EARLY FARMING

The Quakers cleared and plowed fields and cut timber for the first buildings. Slowly the beginnings of a village rose from the landscape – a sawmill,
a flour mill, a large log dwelling, a store, and John's home.

Although the Ellicotts grew wheat, earlier settlers in that area had planted
tobacco for export to England. However, tobacco exhausted the soil, and
after several successive plantings, the land became unproductive. As a result
of this, many Marylanders moved west into Ohio and Kentucky to find new
farmland. However, the Ellicotts learned that through the use of ground
plaster of Paris to fertilize the depleted soils, the land could be made suitable
for growing grain. Thus, the idea for a mill to produce plaster of Paris was
born.

EARLY MILLS

By 1774 the Ellicotts were milling wheat and other grains at their new mill on the east side of the river in Baltimore County. Other farmers in the area also began growing grain and sent their harvests to the Ellicotts for milling.

As farmers prospered, the wheat supply increased; and with the end of the Revolutionary War, the Ellicotts were ready to export their flour. They purchased a waterfront lot in Baltimore and built their first wharf at the corner of Pratt and Light streets.

Locally, the brothers spread their milling operations along the banks of the Patapsco. Joseph, the eldest, lived up the river about two miles and operated the Upper Mills. Andrew and John settled at the Lower Mills, now Ellicott City. Andrew and his sons were responsible for the milling operation. Brother John managed a large store that offered fine goods and furnishings.

By the early 1800s the mills had developed a respected reputation. "Here is one of the largest and most elegant merchant mills in the United States," wrote Joseph Scott in 1807. "It is 100 feet long and 40 feet wide, with four water wheels, which turn three pair of seven feet stones and one of five feet. She is capable of manufacturing 150 barrels of flour in a day. Here also is a

A 1780s sketch by George Ellicott shows the original buildings at Ellicotts Mills. Note the flour mill, sawmill and the waterwheel; these buildings no longer exist.

mill, with one water wheel and a pair of burr stones, for the manufacturing of plaster of Paris. Here likewise is a saw mill and an oil mill which is worked with great spirit." (From *A Geographical Description of the States of Maryland and Delaware*.)

THE ELLICOTTS

The Ellicotts were industrious, inventive, and practical. They developed new methods for milling flour, constructed machine shops, and experimented in farming and technology. This large Quaker family also stressed the importance of education. They brought the best teachers to the community to operate a school for all local children. The Ellicotts attended Meeting (the Quaker religious service) and eventually were instrumental in building a new Quaker meeting house near the mills. After construction of the first mills and workmen's houses in the 1780s, two sons of founder Andrew Ellicott built large stone houses. Jonathan and George chose the east bank of the river, which was near the flour mill, for their large and imposing houses. The homes overlooked the mill race, a man-made canal that provided the water power to operate the mill.

Extensive granite quarries lining the Patapsco River provided the building material for many of the buildings, and in later years, the curbings and

Standing on a grassy knoll by Frederick Road, Jonathan Ellicott's 1780s home is seen here as it was before Hurricane Agnes destroyed it in 1972. Ripped open by debris carried by the raging Patapsco River, the house was subsequently torn down.

walls throughout the old town, and the blocks for the laying of the original railroad tracks. Some of these quarries are still discernible today; one can be seen along Frederick Road where a gas station is located today.

Jonathan Ellicott (1756-1826)

As a young man, Jonathan was caught up in the Revolutionary War. Although Quakers are known for their stand against war, Jonathan became a captain in a militia company but saw no action. He also had manufactured the long swords used by officers of the Maryland Line and the dragoons under the command of Colonel Washington. At the same time, Jonathan was active in the mill operations and was responsible for planning and directing the construction of the road that eventually became the Baltimore-Frederick Turnpike (Route 144). (See Early Roads on page 14.)

George Ellicott (1760-1832)

George Ellicott, according to his daughter, was one of the best mathematicians and finest amateur astronomers of the time. In the publication *Settlement of Ellicott's Mills*, Martha Ellicott Tyson wrote that her father was fond of "imparting instruction to every youthful enquirer after knowledge who came to his house. As early as the year 1782," she wrote, "he was in the habit of giving gratuitous lessons on astronomy to any of the inhabitants of the village who wished to hear him. To many of these his celestial globe was an object of great interest and curiosity. He was perfectly at home on a map

Jonathan and George Ellicott, sons of founder Andrew, built large granite houses in the 1780s. Cousin John's home is to the left. These landmarks remained in place until recently. Jonathan's house was so badly damaged by the 1972 flood that it was razed to the ground. Although George's house survived that flood, it was damaged in the 1975 flood and stood abandoned until 1987, when it was relocated across Frederick Road. The millrace is visible in front of the large stone homes.

of the heavens as far as the telescopes and writers of his time had given revelations." It may be that Benjamin Banneker's interest in astronomy was stimulated by these early sessions.

George Ellicott was also interested in bettering the lives of the American Indian. In 1799 he and other Quakers visited the principal village of the Wyandots in Upper Sandusky, Ohio. Later George and his friend, Gerard Hopkins, made a second trip to instruct the Indians in farming. George was also concerned about the evil affects of alcohol on the American Indian. In 1801 George wrote a letter to Congress asking that the sale of "spiritous liquors" to the Indians be outlawed; such a law was eventually passed.

BENJAMIN BANNEKER (1731-1806)

Benjamin Banneker, a black farmer and astronomer, was born not far from where the Ellicotts built their mills. His mother was a mulatto and his father, a former slave. Banneker had a great intellect and was very learned in mathematics. In fact, he is described as the "first black man of science" in Silvio Bedini's biography, *The Life of Benjamin Banneker.*

Banneker and his father worked 120 acres of land that his father bought with the proceeds from the laborious task of growing tobacco. The younger Banneker was far from being a simple farmer, however. Before he was twenty, he built a wooden clock which struck the hour. In the 1740s, it was

This early and rare photograph, circa the 1850s, shows the mid-19th century Gambrill flour mill with its covered walkway at Ellicotts' Mills. In the foreground, the brick building with three rounded arched windows appears to be the old Granite Manufacturing Company cotton mill. These buildings were extensively damaged in the 1868 flood and never rebuilt. Photograph from the Collection of the Maryland Historical Society, Baltimore.

rare to own a clock, much less build one. This amazing feat brought him local fame. Benjamin became friendly with the Ellicotts, who recognized his ability. In 1790 he accompanied Major Andrew Ellicott to the swamps of the Potomac to lay out the boundaries of the new Federal city, Washington, D.C. George Ellicott had shared his considerable knowledge and equipment with Banneker, enabling him to learn astronomy and publish an almanac for the years 1792-1797.

Benjamin Banneker's original farm on Oella Avenue in Oella, Baltimore County is now being developed into an historical park.

MORE EARLY MILLS

Two other early mills also operated in the close vicinity of the original Ellicotts Mills. Early in the 19th century, the Ellicotts developed a rolling and slitting mill that manufactured iron products, including nails, a most important product for a growing nation. Mendenhall's paper mill was located a short distance down river. Later called the Patapsco or Gray's Mill, it manufactured cotton by 1820. Neither mill now exists.

The present flour mill was constructed after the older mills burned down on May 18, 1918. These buildings housed The Doughnut Corporation of America (DCA). Large silos were added at a later date, after this photograph was taken.

Joseph Atkinson was one of the first settlers to locate a mill on the west side of the river in the present Ellicott City. According to Martha Ellicott Tyson in *Settlement of Ellicott's Mills*, Atkinson leased land from the Ellicotts, and by 1804 he was operating an oil mill and a carding mill for wool. A cotton factory known as the Granite Manufacturing Company stood on the Baltimore

County side of the river, north of the bridge. It was destroyed by the flood of 1868. Oella, a cotton-woolen milling community founded near the beginning of the 19th century, was organized as the Union Manufacturing Company. These original homes that housed workers still stand along Oella Avenue, a winding road to the north, off Route 144. Many of these homes have been lived in continuously to the present day despite the lack of modern facilities, installed in the 1980s.

The Ellicotts remained in the flour-milling business until the 1830s when the Gambrill Company, along with the Carrolls, took over the mill and operated it for nearly 100 years. It was one of three large flour mills which Gambrill owned.

The original Ellicott mills burned about 1805. They were variously rebuilt, enlarged, renovated, and then wiped out by the 1868 flood. The rebuilt mills burned again in the early 20th century. Although the early mills were built of wood, later mills were constructed from fireproof granite. The mills today stand close to where the first mills were located. Although other early buildings have disappeared, a tall brick chimney and a stone building still survive. The mill buildings after World War I were occupied by The Doughnut Corporation of America for almost 50 years, making doughnut machines and doughnut mixes. Today, the milling operation is carried on by the Wilkens Rogers Company, which produces Washington brand baking mixes and products. The company moved here in the early 1970s from Georgetown, near Washington D.C.

After the 1868 flood, the Gambrill Company's flour mill stood amidst the devastation along the Patapsco's shores.

Rear view of the large homes of George (left) and Jonathan Ellicott. Dwarfed by the flour mill buildings, they remained in continual use for nearly two centuries, fronting on the old road. In the 1940s the road was straightened and relocated to the rear of the family homes. Jonathan's home (right) was destroyed by Hurricane Agnes in 1972. George's home was damaged in 1975 by Hurricane Eloise; in 1987 it was moved from its original site to its present location, again facing the road, and now awaits restoration.

OTHER EARLY SURVIVING STRUCTURES

Expansion and growth on the western side of the river developed slowly. According to Quaker minutes, the community built a stone schoolhouse for the children of the neighborhood in the early 1790s. The building, although greatly altered, today serves as the library for the Howard County Historical Society. It is located near the courthouse. A new meeting house was built by 1799, situated on a hill opposite the schoolhouse. The meeting house is now a private home, located above the Columbia Pike.

FIRES AND FLOODS

In 1780 the Ellicott brothers discovered just how treacherous the Patapsco River could be. In that year, a sudden spring thaw nearly destroyed the village. The raging waters swept away the bridge, stables, barns, shops, wagons, carts, horses, and livestock; but miraculously, no lives were lost. Succeeding generations were not so lucky.

The flood of July 24, 1868 started with a light rain. After eighteen inches had fallen in the western valley of the Patapsco, the gentle summer rain turned into a menace; soon flood waters churned through Ellicott City and destroyed bridges, factories, homes, and lives. Families had previously experienced the rising of the river into the first floor of their homes, but this was much worse. As the river continued to rise, the residents climbed higher and higher in their houses, finally clinging to the roofs. But there was no escape from the raging waters; 36 persons died as friends and relatives watched helplessly.

Before the 1868 flood, the area between the railroad and the Patapsco River had a different appearance. Buildings stood on both sides of the turn-pike road. An 1860 newspaper described Talbott's lumberyard, Bradley's store, and a stone house on the north side of the road. On the opposite side of the road near the tracks were a number of structures: a brick building, a tin and stove store operated by Collier, a frame house used as a store by John Blackhead, a store occupied by John Kavanaugh, and Coombs' shoemaker shop. All but one of these structures were lost. Only the stone house on the north side of the road still stands.

By 1878 W. W. Radcliffe owned this stone house where he operated a coal and lumberyard business. Other businesses or organizations that used the building were the Bridge Market, The Church of God, Clark's coal yard and lawn mower services, and Appalachian Outfitters. After the disastrous flood

In 1975 Hurricane Eloise brought torrential rains which caused the Patapsco River to overflow into lower Main Street.

At the turn of the 20th century, an elevated walkway connected the two mills at Ellicott City. To the left are two stone homes built by the Ellicotts and the millrace, which was subsequently filled in to create additional parking for cars.

of 1972, the building stood near ruin before its recent renovation as an office, with a county parking lot to the rear. The buildings destroyed in the 1868 flood were never replaced. Today, it is difficult to visualize the many additional structures at this location.

Flooding has occurred repeatedly through the years. A third "hundred years' flood" came in the form of Hurricane Agnes in 1972. The raging river tore out the concrete bridge over the Patapsco and ripped open the 190-year-old stone house of Jonathan Ellicott. In 1975 Hurricane Eloise filled up lower Main Street like a large basin, and the shops were again inundated with water to the second story.

George's home, built in 1789, was badly damaged by the flood of 1975. The house stood empty and deteriorating for a dozen years before it was skillfully moved across the road, above the flood plain. It is the sole remaining structure from the early Ellicotts Mills 18th century community.

EARLY ROADS

When the Ellicotts first came to the "Hollow," they had to ford the Patapsco River because there was no bridge. It was not long, however, before they built a wooden bridge. More than a bridge was needed if the farmers were to bring grain to the Ellicotts' mill. The Ellicotts built and funded a road to Doughoregan Manor, owned by Charles Carroll of Carrollton, signer of the Declaration of Independence. Carroll sent his wheat to the mill and lent the millers money for their operation. The Ellicotts engineered and built the extension of the road westward to Fredericktown in the 1790s. Landowners along the way contributed to the cost of construction.

Road building was quite an undertaking in those times. As recorded in *American Family History* (edited by Harry and Charlotte Hoffman), the Ellicotts "built a house on wheels which was drawn from place to place by horses, being the first movable building seen in Maryland; it contained conveniences for cooking everything but bread, which was always baked and forwarded from the Mills, from the kitchen of John Ellicott, one of the members of the firm..."

The road the Ellicotts built to Fredericktown later became a part of the National Road, also called the Cumberland Road (today's Route 40). The idea for a National Road took shape while Thomas Jefferson was President (1801-1809). Thomas B. Searight in *The Old Pike* credits Albert Gallatin, Jefferson's Treasury Secretary, with the idea for such a road. He confirms that "the connecting link between Cumberland and the city of Baltimore is a road much older than the Cumberland Road, constructed and owned by associations of individuals and the two together constitute the National Road."

A covered bridge replaced the Ellicotts' wooden bridge; it likely was repaired and replaced many times. When the covered bridge burned on June 7, 1914, it was replaced with a new concrete bridge. Fifty-eight years later,

Looking into Baltimore County, one sees the old covered and trolley bridges as they stood side by side. In 1850 local citizens petitioned the state legislature to ban cattle drives through Ellicotts Mills on Sunday mornings. The thundering animals endangered citizens crossing the covered bridge en route to church.

In this photo from the early 1900s, the Oliver Viaduct which carried the B&O across Main Street had not yet had two of its arches removed. The old hotel stood abandoned and weakened at this time, leading to the collapse of the structure in the 1920s. Note the billboard advertisement for the Pontiac automobile priced at $825.

Hurricane Agnes ripped it from its foundations. Another bridge was built and it survived Hurricane Eloise in 1975.

The Oliver Viaduct, originally a three-arched bridge, carried the B&O railroad across the Frederick Turnpike. The bridge was named after Robert Oliver, Esquire, a leading Baltimore merchant and a member of the first B&O Board of Directors. His country estate stood where the Greenmount Cemetery in Baltimore is now located. After the advent of the trolley, the resulting traffic jams and accidents along Main Street led to the removal of two of the bridge's arches to facilitate the flow of traffic.

THE CIVIL WAR (1861-1865)

Families recount that mixed loyalties prevailed in Howard County during the Civil War, with Ellicott City citizens generally supporting the North. However, farmers did hide their horses in the woods to prevent the Union troops from taking them. Other families had members who took money and supplies south to the Confederate troops. The Northern soldiers were aware of these activities and sought to capture Southern sympathizers, often without success. The local people were too clever with their hiding places or disguises. In fact, one family even buried their silver plate in a manure pile to keep it safe from the Yankees.

Excitement heightened during the war when Union troops recaptured the Winans Steam Gun in Ellicotts Mills in May 1861. *The Baltimore Sun* recorded

The trolley bridge was completed in 1899 and stood until it was dismantled in 1955. The concrete bridge was built after the 1914 fire which destroyed the covered wooden one. It was destroyed by Hurricane Agnes in June 1972 and was replaced in record time; by October of that year, a new concrete bridge was built which withstood the ravages of Hurricane Eloise three years later. Note the double porches on the stone building (8000 Main Street).

the story soon after the event. Union forces discovered that Southern sympathizers were taking an experimental centrifugal steam gun from Baltimore to Harper's Ferry, through Ellicotts Mills. Naturally such a weapon would even the odds for the South, as the North had more men. The gun's inventor, Charles Dickinson, described the operation of his new weapon:

> "Rendered ball-proof, and protected by an iron cone, and mounted on a four-wheel carriage, it can be readily moved from place to place or kept on march with an army. It can be constructed to discharge missiles of any capacity from an ounce ball to a twenty-four pound shot, with a force and range equal to the most approved gunpowder projectiles, and can discharge from one hundred to five hundred balls per minute."

When the Union forces heard that the gun would be taken through Ellicotts Mills, General Benjamin Butler boarded a B&O train with several hundred men and headed to the town. The troops captured the gun, mules, and the three men in charge of the operation. But Dickinson carried the vital

Early 20th century Main Street had plenty of room for horse-drawn vehicles. Wooden water pumps, locally made by businessman Hamilton Oldfield, were placed along the street to provide water for the saddle and harness horses that brought people to town.

parts separately from the weapon and escaped in a buggy, rendering the gun useless. The captured gun was taken to the Union encampment at Relay and never fired.

A Union Soldier's Story Of Ellicotts Mills

According to research by Philip Reitzel, in 1864 a sixteen-year-old enlistee named Louis LeClear longed to be part of a twelve-man detail sent to Ellicotts Mills. He was stationed at Relay House, in the Elkridge vicinity, six miles east on the B&O line, and soon got his wish. Through correspondence, we learn that young Louis came to the town in August 1864. Louis writes that the provost marshall, a Captain Brown, and the soldiers occupied "the fourth and fifth stories of a large building originally intended for a Free Mason's Lodge." (This is the building at 8044 Main Street, once known as the New Town Hall). Their principal duty was "to put a guard of one man at the door of a big room in the highest story of the house in which we are stationed to see that none of the prisoners we have there escape. They consist of 'Sesesh' [Confederate or pro-secession] prisoners brought here to stay over night for want of transportation, of drafted men who overstaid their ten days and of deserters."

LeClear wrote that fruit was cheap. Splendid big peaches were 35 cents a peck and big watermelons, 20 cents. What particularly caught his eye were the girls who worked in the cloth mills. He also described the drovers who brought large herds of mules through town. Two or three hundred mules would follow the lead of a gray mare with a bell on her neck, ridden by the drover. Louis wrote his parents that government rations were salt beef, hard tack, and beans. However, they would "draw" potatoes from a field about a mile from town. They also had all the fox grapes, apples, or peaches they wanted.

MAIN STREET FROM 1900

As part of the Western Turnpike, Main Street took on added importance. By 1900 the trolley carried passengers up and down the street. At one time there were two lines of tracks – to and from the terminus at Fells Lane. The Ellicott City Trolley Line extended from Fells Lane to the Catonsville junction.

However, as the number of automobiles increased, the resulting traffic created a problem for trolley operations. Jean Holmes, a former editor of *The Ellicott City Times*, wrote in the 1972 Bicentennial Journal that the discussion of "Who's blocking the street car?" became an almost daily ritual. Unless cars were parked with their tires rubbing the curb, the street car could not get by. According to Holmes, "the ritual began with the frantic clanging of the trolley bell. Then a blue-uniformed conductor would dash in and out of stores bellowing, 'Whose blue Ford is blocking the street car?' If the owner did not appear fishing for his keys as the trolley men glared, the next ritual step was 'rocking the car.'

"Assisted by those drawn by the clanging and bellowing (although the residents were not surprised at the ritual, they always gathered to enjoy it), the motorman and conductor would rock the car hoping to move it toward the curb. If all else failed, a furious motorman would change the handle from one end of the trolley to the other and go barreling back to Baltimore, perhaps leaving a handful of potential patrons waiting at the terminus."

The trolley tracks have long since become a part of the past, and the granite Belgian blocks were taken up in the 1920s. Gone too are the trees that once shaded the thoroughfare, and Mr. Oldfield's wooden water troughs that stood along the street. The water pumps were part of an early public water system that was supplied from a reservoir on the hill.

Main Street was U.S. Route 40 until a wider Route 40 was built north of town in the 1940s.

ELLICOTT CITY GOVERNMENT

Howard County, officially established on July 4, 1851, was named to honor John Eager Howard, a hero of the Revolutionary War and Maryland's fifth governor. Before that it had been designated as "Howard District" of Anne Arundel County in 1839. Previously the region was known as "upper Anne Arundel County."

When granted a city charter in 1867, Ellicotts Mills changed its name to Ellicott City. The incorporated town was governed first by a mayor and council, then later by a city commission. George Ellicott Jr., grandson of founder Andrew, was selected as the first mayor. Thomas McCrea furnished the first mayor's office, and the council met at I. Wolfersberger's, a local merchant. According to the minutes of the council proceedings, one of the first acts of the local government was to order a corporate seal "for the use of the Mayor and Council [and] two books for the registrar to record the proceedings of the Council and the Ordinances of the City." They also purchased "a lamp and oil."

In 1914 the commission form of government was adopted, and the town's boundaries were changed. Originally the town incorporated parts of Baltimore County; but in 1914 the Patapsco River became the dividing line.

The trolley stands front and center on lower Main Street; O'Brien's business is only a one-story building at this time. Later Mr. Fissell added a second floor in the 1920s. Today the building houses the Phoenix Restaurant.

Parades through town were very popular. Here Sergeant Walter Carter leads the Maryland Minutemen in the 1943 Memorial Day parade as they climb up the hill past the corner at Columbia Pike. The question has been raised, why did the parades march uphill, rather than follow the more logical and easier route downhill to the river.

After 1935 Ellicott City became unincorporated, joining other county towns that chose county government rule. The *Times* reported that the town could operate on a very small real estate tax base because there was a high license fee for saloons. Prohibition (1920-1933) eliminated much of the town's revenue, and the ensuing tax increases were the cause of many bitter protests that finally led to the surrender of the town charter.

SINCE WORLD WAR II

Time has greatly changed this historic mill town. Until the 1950s, local shops provided the necessities for day-to-day living. Merchants kept shelves well stocked for those who came to town, particularly on Saturdays when the shopkeepers stayed open as long as a customer was there. Ellicott City, as the county seat, fairly bustled as the social and business center of the county. Here one caught the trolley into Catonsville or Baltimore. You went west by train or, in the early days, by stagecoach. There were several livery stables to keep the horses when you rode or drove into town.

World War II ushered in more changes. Saloons seemed to occupy nearly half of the Main Street buildings. Outsiders moved to town to work at the mills, and military men found their way into the once quiet village. Change continued after the war ended. Returning veterans sought more modern surroundings, and many families moved away. Most could now afford automobiles. Soon shopping centers appeared, and as merchants left Main Street their customers followed.

The transitional years in the 1960s saw the town take on a new face as antique dealers found the town a fitting background for their wares, and speciality merchants were attracted by the low rents and quaint facades. Although Hurricane Agnes struck a devastating blow to the town in 1972, it was a catalyst for renewal. Ellicott City was planning its Bicentennial festivities that fall, and the cooperation and efforts of so many people, determined to rebuild the town, brought about a successful celebration that propelled the town toward a sound future.

Main Street,
North Side

MAIN STREET OVERVIEW

Main Street developed as a commercial center, despite the steep hills rising from the river and the imposing blocks of granite bulging from the hillsides. Note how the buildings on the north side of the street are built directly against huge granite rocks. These buildings reflect the values of the people who built them. In the early 1800s, many of the settlers were Quakers, as were the Ellicott brothers. They were unpretentious, humble, and practical. When they constructed their buildings, they used locally available materials; there was plenty of wood and granite as well as rubble stone. These buildings were sturdy and plain with little ornamentation. In contrast, later buildings reflect a more decorative, Victorian style of architecture. Styles of the early 20th century are evident in most of the brick structures.

THE MYSTERY OF THE LOTTERY AND THE PATAPSCO HOTEL

In 1831 the Ellicotts sold a half-block parcel on the north side of Main Street to Andrew McLaughlin for $16,000 and held the $11,000 mortgage on the property. Two years later McLaughlin received General Assembly approval to hold a lottery to dispose of his estate. It is difficult to imagine the reasons for this lottery. Had McLaughlin over-extended himself financially? Did he have to sell this property to pay his debts? Was he seeking new business ventures elsewhere? Whatever the reason, it is not recorded, but a lottery poster survives and paints a glowing picture of Ellicott City in 1834:

> "One of the most romantic, healthy and prosperous villages in the United States, admired by every passing traveller and celebrated for its great manufacturing advantages. The clink of the hammer is heard from every quarter, splitting the gray granite, which abounds in inexhaustible

quantities; the dull noise of the forges and rapid motion of Saw Mills; the hum of ten thousand spindles in the Cotton Factories, the whirl of the many mill stones, and the white spray of the pure water which is constantly tumbling over the dam, mingling with the cheerful bustle of the industrious and enterprising villagers, give the whole scene a most animating character and make it the happy resort of thousands of admiring visitors."

The poster also describes details of the lottery. For $10 a ticket, you could purchase a chance on many prizes such as a bottle of champagne, a marble mantle clock, a large mahogany sideboard, or a valuable building lot. The first prize was land valued at $36,000. According to the poster, there were several lots. Lot No. 1 "upon which are erected the extensive improvements known as the Patapsco Hotel, with the New Addition upon the RailRoad, and the large and highly ornamental Garden of nearly three acres. Lot No. 25 upon which are erected the large stone stables and carriage house. Lot No. 24, being the Ice House lot." The poster further boasted that $3,000 yearly

VALUABLE REAL AND PERSONAL PROPERTY
BY
LOTTERY,

This 1834 lottery poster depicts early Ellicotts Mills as the town matured on the west side of the Patapsco River. In the background, left to right, are Mount Ida, the Patapsco Female Institute, and Angelo's Cottage. The buildings on Main Street, beginning at the left, are 8060, 8048-56, and 8044-46; the empty lot is 8030-34; and the large building adjacent to the railroad tracks was part of the Patapsco Hotel. The connecting walkway permitted pedestrians to walk above Main Street which was often odoriferous and muddy or dusty. In the right foreground is the railroad depot — note the doors on the end of the building. Behind the Hotel the train begins its westward journey. The smokestacks indicate the factories close to town. Photograph courtesy of the Peale Museum of Baltimore.

rent had been recently offered for the hotel. We know today that this first prize, valued at $36,000, included what later became four distinct properties. They started adjacent to the railroad tracks and extended through the row of five narrow brick buildings as far as 8056 Main Street. Today the properties are (1) the old Patapsco Hotel, adjacent to the tracks; (2) the Railroad Hotel; (3) the Town Hall; and (4) the five brick buildings. But even with the poster's description of the first prize, there are still questions about the buildings that remain unanswered. The main puzzle centers on the location of the original Patapsco Hotel. Was it the structure adjacent to the railroad track, or might it have been the old stone building west of the tracks? Is it possible that the "New Addition upon the Rail Road," as stated on the poster, was a totally separate building, as the lottery picture shows? Were the extensive improvements known as the Patapsco Hotel, in fact, 8044-46 Main Street – the Opera House/Town Hall?

In Scott's *1807 Geographical Description*, there was mention of "a good tavern, for the accommodation of travellers, and others" at Ellicott's Lower Mills. McLaughlin may have taken this old stone tavern, made extensive improvements to it, renamed it the Patapsco Hotel, and connected it by wooden sidewalks to the "New Addition upon the railroad." We know the railroad used the new addition for passengers who entered the facilities directly from the tracks as there were no waiting rooms in the early stone station.

The tallest building in town has had many names: New Town Hall, Rodey's Amusea, and the Opera House.

Joseph Barling of Baltimore City held ticket No. 5086 and claimed first prize. The property was deeded to him in February 1835. In September he took out a loan from the American Life Insurance Company for $5,000, mortgaging the property. He leased the right to quarry stone in the garden the same year. But Barling too got into financial difficulties. The court appointed John H. B. Latrobe as trustee, and he sold the property for about $9,000 to the Granite Manufacturing Company. According to John McGrain in *From Pig Iron to Cotton Duck*, the investors at Granite bought the hotel for company housing to accommodate journeymen machinists and iron workers.

In 1847 Thomas Wilson bought the property. During this period John R. Brown operated the hotel, and it was called Brown's Hotel by the local citizens. In 1850 the *Gazette* described an addition to the hotel that included a lady's parlor, twelve chambers, and a spacious entrance from Main Street which was connected to the enlarged center hall of the Hotel. After the Civil War McGowan operated the hotel until 1877 when the building was again advertised for sale or rent; by this time Thomas Wilson was located in Baltimore. During the next few years a portion of the property (8004-26 Main Street) changed hands when Thomas Hunt bought it for $4,000 in 1881. In 1887 the building became a printing facility where *The Ellicott City Times* was published. In the early 1900s it was converted to an ice house, and many of the supporting girders were removed to accommodate more ice. In the 1920s a railroad engine jumped the tracks and struck the old structure, weakening it still further. By April 1926, the aging historic building had collapsed. Owner Pennington, a Baltimore businessman, tore it down and rebuilt it to its present day form.

8000 Main Street: D. W. Taylor, Architect/Planner

This solitary building between the railroad and the river once was one of several buildings that were demolished in the 1868 flood. At that time, this was a dwelling. W. W. Radcliff owned it in 1878 and sold food, clothing, coal, wood, and lime. In 1887 one side was a dwelling and the other, a general store. In this century it has held the Bridge Market, Church of God, part of Clark's Hardware, and Appalachian Outfitters. Hurricane Agnes in 1972 severely damaged the building, which then stood empty for more than ten years before restoration in the mid-1980s.

Pictured left is the one remaining building of the several that were originally located here; the others were swept away in the 1868 flood.

8004-26 Main Street: Deeds Book Shop, Humpty-Dumpty, Dandyline Fashions, Kitchen Basket, and F & R Antiques

Since the hotel's reconstruction in the 1920s, the upper floors have been used as apartments with a variety of shops at street level.

8030-34 Main Street: Caryl Maxwell Ballet, New Covenant Faith Fellowship, Upper Room, Concantenations, and The Mine Shaft

The 1834 lottery poster shows this parcel as a vacant lot. Today it is called the Railroad Hotel, but it may actually be the 1850 addition to the old Patapsco Hotel. In 1860 Voltz had a tailor shop in the building, and Mellon operated a store at street level. By 1887 the building housed a barber, a tailor, an office, and dwellings on the upper levels. Ed Rodey bought this property in 1912 for $1500. Early 20th century businesses included a shoemaker, a barber, and a lodge on the top floor.

8044-46 Main Street: Jonathan Ellicott's Marketplace, housing the Forget-me-not Factory

Note how close the building is to the granite hillside. On the second floor, the rear wall is formed by the granite rock itself. A portion of this building may have been the 1807 tavern mentioned previously in Scott's 1807 description of Ellicotts Mills. It was part of the sale and resale of the hotel property until it was owned by Thomas Wilson, who leased it in 1857 to John Schofield for $75 a year for a ten-year period. If Schofield had wished to purchase it instead, the price would have been $1,250. In 1858 Schofield borrowed $2,000 from Centre Lodge No. 40 of the Independent Order of Odd Fellows for building improvements. The Lodge also had space here. Schofield operated the Patapsco Enterprise Offices and enlarged the four-story building by adding a fifth floor of brick and a vertical addition that enclosed a stairway. The 1860 map of Howard County by Simon J. Martenet, a well-known surveyor and Maryland mapmaker, was printed at his offices. Because Schofield received financial support from the commissioners, he was required to give a copy of the map to each public school. The building was named "the new Town Hall" after the top floor was built and used as the Town Hall.

In 1867 Wilson sold this property, separate from the hotel property, to Michael Bannon for $1250. In 1882 Wolfersberger published the *American Progress* newspaper every Friday. This periodical, oriented toward the Republican Party, was published from 1871 to 1889. From 1890 to 1896, and

The trolley traveled as far as the fire station on Main Street before reversing direction to return to Catonsville. The roadster with passengers in the rumble seat gives evidence of a fine summer day. Photograph courtesy of Robert M. Vogel.

possibly longer, the newspaper was called the *Howard County Progress.* Holzman and Fridenwald also manufactured ladies' underwear here, employing 50 young women at wages of $2 to $6 per week. Later, the Oppenheim, Obendorf and Company shirt factory occupied the lower floors of the building. The company eventually expanded to a new building on Fells Lane, two blocks west. School groups and others performed in the new Town Hall located on the top floor.

In the early 1900s Ed Rodey bought the building. It was known for a time as Rodey's Amusea, where customers could enjoy silent movies and arcade-style games. In 1922 *The Ellicott City Times* advertised a Halloween barn dance at Rodey's Amusea – ladies 50 cents, gents 75 cents. The upper floors at one time were converted to apartments.

Other building tenants have included Bill Hood's Grocery, Yates' Grocery, and Ecklof's Furniture Store.

8048-56 Main Street: Lela's Balkan Art, Crystal Underground, Ruthie's Rhapsody, Wood'N Nickel, and Capt. K's

This row of brick buildings, which has held a variety of shops through the years, was the fourth section of Lot 1 of the lottery first prize. In 1865 Wilson sold this part of Lot 1 to the Granite Manufacturing Company for $3,500. Seven years later George Feelemyer bought it for the same price.

Tragedy struck one shopowner in 1895. Daniel F. Shea, who kept a tobacco store in a room next to the old town hall, was found murdered, lying in a pool of blood. A young black man was soon arrested, and he confessed to the crime. The jury deliberated just twenty minutes before returning a guilty verdict. About two weeks before the young man was to be hanged, a lynch mob took him from the jail and marched him up the lane past the Patapsco Institute where they hanged him from a dogwood tree. Many in the community felt that the young man's guilty verdict might have been reversed. Since he had been examined by doctors, there were suspicions that he was mentally incompetent. Although the lynch mob had been hooded, it was believed that they were Ellicott City citizens.

These buildings were called "brick row" on Wilson's plat of the early 1900s. The properties were owned by the Wosch and Kroh families for a period of time, and after that ownership changed many times.

8060 Main Street: Alda Baptiste

This stone and frame building is one of the early structures from old Ellicotts Mills. Although it has been altered over the years, its shape and foundation are approximately the same as it was in 1833. In fact, Lot 2 in the 1834 lottery listed this property as a new three-story dwelling with a hewn-granite basement. According to the poster, the building was valued at $3,000. Robert Campbell of Baltimore City held winning ticket No. 90. In 1865 Robert Campbell Jr. sold the property to Elizabeth Laumann for $2,000; it was then called the "Laumann Building." In 1877 Daniel Laumann advertised as a dealer in green groceries, fruits, and provisions, with fresh and cool lager beer always on hand. In 1887 the building was used as a residence. It later became the Ecklof Furniture Store. In 1908 Mrs. Dorothy Kraft bought the property at a public sale for $1,800, and it remained in the Kraft family until 1945.

8066-74 Main Street: Cacao Lane

These properties, Lots 3 and 4 in the 1834 lottery, were valued at $750 each. They sold in 1843 for $1,000 and $900, respectively. Portions of these two three-story houses are over 150 years old; the simple cut-stone and frame construction is common in the town. The building has held many businesses over its 100 years.

Early owners included Elizabeth Hunt who operated a millinery shop in one section and Thomas Hunt who sold dry goods and groceries in the other.

The Hunt family held the properties until the 1920s. Later uses included a bar, taxi-cab company, and a pool room.

Note that there is a three-foot-wide alley between the units on the lower level. A number of buildings on the north side of Main Street have such alleyways, some with gardens in the rear. These alleyways provided access to deliverymen and servants.

8076 Main Street: *Newly added as part of Cacao Lane*

This parcel was Lot 5 in the lottery drawing and was won by William Cowland of Baltimore with ticket No. 5624. James Mathews, the postmaster in 1886, operated a store at this location. He was also an agent for the Mutual Fire Insurance Company in 1879. The stone building, three and one-half stories tall, was built in the 1830s; note the single center dormer.

8080 Main Street: *Esprit de Corps*

This site, with the original dwelling, was Lot 6 in the 1834 lottery. Samuel Ellicott won this prize, and in 1837 he leased it to Mary Duvall for $33 per year. She lived in the building and operated a millinery shop. Under the long-term lease arrangement, Mrs. Duvall was responsible for the taxes and upkeep of the property, and the lease continued until her death nearly 60 years later. At that time, the property was sold at auction in 1900 for $800. In 1935 Norman Moxley bought the site, tore down the building, and built the present structure for a shop with three apartments upstairs. Moxley, who had a successful building and plastering business, later went into politics and land development. For many years Bob Weigel's five-and-dime store was located here.

8086 Main Street: *Perfect Color Photo Service*

The 1834 lottery apparently attracted attention far beyond Ellicotts Mills. Lot 7 was won by John Williams of Deerfield, Massachusetts with ticket No. 4792. He was deeded the property, probably a vacant lot, in August 1835. It, along with the one west of it, was bought by Nathaniel Ellicott; at his death in 1839 the land was put on the auction block. In 1849 the Talbotts bought the two lots plus a lot in the rear for $500. By 1887 records showed a two-story dwelling on the property. Through the years the building has been altered and used as the Heaveys' residence, a restaurant and tavern, the Old Line Antique Shop, and law offices.

Pictured here on the left is the Bankers Galleria (formerly a bank and now housing shops) and right, the Margaret Smith Gallery.

8090 Main Street: Margaret Smith Gallery

This was the last of the 1834 lottery properties. Philip Earlougher of Baltimore City won with lucky ticket No. 900 and received the deed in April 1835. It was one of the lots purchased by the Talbotts mentioned above. They sold this property to the Patapsco Bank in 1886 for $1,800; the bank then relocated to Main Street from its location on the hill near St. Paul Street. J. J. Norton bought the building for his drug store when he acquired Dr. Martin's pharmacy business. Ben Mellor operated the Patapsco Pharmacy here until it moved to 8181 Main Street. When the Zito Brothers operated Rock Hill Liquors, the facade was altered to appear more modern, with the addition of two show windows and a center door. The building has since been restored to its original design.

8098 Main Street: Bankers Galleria, housing Scoop du Jour, Lomal Calligraphy, Victoria Bear, Quilt Factory, and Joni's Heart Strings

Originally in 1887 a tin shop operated from one lot on this property, and the other lot held a livery stable. The Hunts held the property for approximately 50 years before selling to the Patapsco Bank in 1903. The old buildings were torn down, and the New Patapsco Bank was built in 1905, moving from next door (8090 Main Street). The Patapsco Bank became the First National Bank before closing its doors in the 1980s.

When the bank was built, a local newspaper reported "one of the most attractive features of the building is the room set aside for ladies doing

The interior of the Patapsco Bank at 8098 Main Street in its early days. The original cornice and window moldings can still be seen, and the vault remains in one of the first floor shops. The green Italian marble tabletops of the teller cages are from a later era. The bench in the photograph is now with the Howard County Historical Society, a gift of Ben Mellor, a long-time bank associate.

business with the bank. This has been fitted up in a very attractive manner with writing desks, stationery, chairs, etc., a fine old colonial fireplace and toilet room adjoining." Constructed in the neo-colonial style, the building is three bays wide and one story tall with a gabled roof and Doric columns. Note the quoins or large squared stones on the corners of the building. This architectural feature provides a sense of stability and strength, important assets to a bank.

8104 Main Street: (Lot 138 on Ellicott plat)

For the sum of $25, August Wallenhorst leased the property in 1864 from Caleb Dorsey. If purchased, the lot would have cost $500. Property values apparently increased slightly in the next few years, because records show that Augusta Wosch bought the lot for $574.20 in 1871. It is unknown when this structure was built; according to old maps, there was a frame building on the site by 1878. It was probably used as a jewelry store, since that is known to have been there by 1887.

The store became a setting for romance around 1914. At that time Isaac Taylor had just bought Leo Rosenfeld's jewelry and optical business and set up shop in the store. From here, young Isaac would hear lovely violin music coming from across the street where Rose Caplan was practicing her lessons. They met and found the attraction was mutual. Although Taylor moved his store three times before constructing a new building on the corner, these responsibilities did not deter the courtship and marriage of the young couple.

Later store owners included Andrew Kraft in 1918 and the Burgesses in 1955. Other uses were office of the town's police chief, Julius Wosch; Burgess Insurance; the American Red Cross; and the Ross Barber Shop.

8116 Main Street: Maxine's Potpourri (Lot 139 on Ellicott plat)

In 1865 Caleb Dorsey leased the parcel to Henry Henke for $25 a year, and Dorothy Kraft purchased it in 1894. The building was then owned by Isidore and Nellie Meyer and Sam Caplan. The Peddicord's appliance store operated here before moving across the street.

The Italianate brick building was probably built before 1887. Note the ornate lintels over the windows of the second and third stories and the attractive bracketing under the eaves.

8120 Main Street: Santa Fe Way (Lot 140 on Ellicott plat)

This property was sold in 1856 for $300, in 1868 for $800, and in 1891 for $1,500. In 1887 a two-story building where house furnishings were sold was listed on the site. It was likely a prosperous business, because early 20th century pictures show it as a three-story building.

In 1893 you could walk into Abe Cohen's clothing store and buy an all-wool suit that was worth $9 for $4.50. He also advertised "good everyday" pants for 75 cents.

Isaac Taylor moved his jewelry and optical shop here in 1915 after buying the building for $3,000. In 1937 John Votta purchased the building from Anna Navicki, a widow whose husband had been a shoemaker. Votta came from Little Italy in Baltimore with his young wife to open his own shoe repair shop. When he served as county sheriff in the 1970s, he leased his business.

Note that the first two stories of the stucco-covered brick building are constructed directly against the solid granite at the rear. There is a walk-out door at the rear of the third floor.

8126 Main Street: Owl and Pussy Cat, Odd Fellows Lodge

In 1848 these lots, 141-145, were purchased by Isaiah Mercer for $625. G. F. Hess had a harness shop there until 1860, when the Independent Order of Odd Fellows (IOOF) purchased the building for $2,000. An adjacent older frame building had previously served as the IOOF Hall, where The Centre Lodge No. 40, IOOF was instituted in March 1843. According to the *Times*, nearly every family in the area was listed as a charter member. In the early days, when a member was ill, other members served as nurses and sometimes stayed through the night.

The granite 3-1/2 story building was probably built as early as the 1850s and is still in use today by the Odd Fellows.

8156 Main Street: Fishbein and Fishbein

In 1887 a frame building on this site used as a drug warehouse was owned by Dr. Isaac Martin, a pharmacist and ordained minister. According to land records, the building was used as a laboratory. Martin died in 1893. At one time, a small frame building adjacent to the laboratory was used by the "colored" barber, Frank Scott. Dr. Martin's heir, Roswell Martin, sold the property in 1903 for $1,500. *The Democratic Journal,* under the ownership of William Powell, eventually had offices in the building. Powell took over *The Ellicott City Times* in 1905, which was later managed by Edward B. Powell. The newspaper was sold in 1920 to Paul G. Stromberg, who gradually purchased all of the stock in the Maryland Printing and Publishing Company, which had controlled the paper since 1913.

This early frame building was replaced by a brick structure around 1926. An open lot with interesting granite boulders stands to the west.

The present building was constructed in

1926 by the Maryland Printing and Publishing Company. In its next brush
with history, the building presented firemen with a challenge during a fire at
the site on January 11, 1940. At that time, the U.S. Post Office and the Melville
Scott and Sons Insurance Company shared occupancy with *The Times*. When
the firemen arrived, they found a car parked in front of the hydrant. They
had to open the front doors of the car and run the hose through the vehicle!
According to B. Harrison Shipley's *History of the Fire Department*, no mail was
damaged in the blaze. Unfortunately, however, old editions of the
newspaper stored under a staircase that burned were destroyed.

8180 Main Street: Ellicotts Country Store (Lot 121, 1839 division of George Ellicott's property)

The property was leased in 1833 by Samuel Ellicott to A. E. Walker for
$50 per year. Leases in the early 1800s were generally for 99 years. The lessee
also paid all assessments, taxes, and public dues. However, if the yearly rent
was in arrears for 60 days, the lessor could repossess the property until the
rent was paid. If no payments were made for one year, the owner could
permanently repossess it.

By 1855 Henry Chandler of Washington was advertising his new country
store in *The Gazette*. He bought the building in 1864 for $2,425. It was also
known as the Kinsey Building. Isaiah Kinsey made, repaired, and sold boots,
shoes, and gaiters. Gaiters, also known as leggings, were made of either cloth
or leather.

Twentieth-century businesses included undertaker Frank Higinbothom,
Bloom's Bar, Stonesifer Restaurant, and Yates Record Shop.

This building is another example of the early granite-block structures
popular in Ellicotts Mills.

8186-88 Main Street: Heirlooms (Lot 147 on Jonathan Ellicott's plat)

This building is made up of two identical brick houses with crushed-
marble veneers. The houses were probably built about 1840. The ownership
of the property provides us with a mystery. The building was purchased in
1842 by Marcus Denison, trustee, for the benefit of Charlotte Tazewell.
According to the land records, the property was for her use "free of all control
whatever" from her present or future husband. Oliver Tazewell, her
husband, was well-known in the community. He advertised in 1840 that he

sold and repaired watches and locks. Was he irresponsible or did perhaps Charlotte's family disapprove of the marriage?

In 1887, one half of the building was used for a boot and shoe store, and the other half was a bank. Later uses included Bud Gray's Barber Shop and a beauty shop.

8198 Main Street: Residence

This 3-1/2 story building, one room deep, was constructed in 1835. It is one of the oldest houses on the north side of Main Street. As is true throughout the town, the granite buildings were little altered from their original construction. They were sturdy, amply proportioned, and required no major exterior alterations.

Samuel Ellicott leased the building in 1835 to Samuel R. Powell for $34.50 per year for the standard lease period of 99 years. In 1887, the house was used as a confectionary. Eliza Thomas occupied the house in 1897 and found she had a good neighbor. When the hotel next door was renovated, the hotel owner agreed to install a new roof and rain pipes, and to add a brick wall for

The Howard House Hotel (8200 Main) was a smaller structure in the 19th century. This early photo shows the three-story building with three dormers. The frame building to the left was torn down for the new addition. Directly above the old hotel was the Methodist parsonage, now gone.

Eliza's use. In 1939 the building was owned by the Hoplite Club, a men's athletic organization.

8202 Main Street: Howard House – under renovation

James Shipley built a structure here about 1840. Land records report the property was sold in 1842 for the use of Harriett Shipley, wife of James, for $1,000. The property was auctioned later that year for $1,800 to William Worthington. He could not make the payments, so in 1843 the hotel was again put on the auction block. Thomas Anderson bought it for $1,545 at a sale conducted by Sheriff Isaac Anderson. Thomas then leased it to George Bond, who was the town postmaster from 1855-1858. Josiah Groves, who operated the hotel, purchased it in 1865 for $2,500. Groves became well known in the community. When he first arrived in town in 1850, he had advertised his experience as a wheelwright and coachmaker. He said he had worked in the best factories in Philadelphia. Later Groves and his son W.

The Howard House Hotel was converted to an apartment house in the 20th century. A second-story wrought-iron porch and shutters were part of the handsome facade of the aging stone building.

Dall had a real estate business in town. After the Civil War, they also ran the Union Hotel (8298-8304 Main Street) and renamed it the City Hotel.

In 1879 the Howard House again went up for public sale. Christian Eckert bought the building for $5,680; although he initially faced problems, he became one of the building's more successful owners. For a period of time during Eckert's tenure, a local option law closed the bar, creating a financial hardship. To compensate, Eckert produced ice cream, soda water, and ginger ale. Near the turn of the century, he made major improvements to the property by enlarging the original building and adding the large granite building attached to the west (8210 Main Street). Tradition says the dining room of the hotel was so popular that the new building was added to accommodate more patrons. It is also said that the public used Howard House to climb the hill from Main Street to the Court House by taking a shortcut through the hotel. The Eckerts welcomed the traffic; they correctly anticipated that visitors would be enticed into the dining room by the inviting aromas wafting from the kitchen. Ownership of the building changed many times in the 1900s. In recent years there have been apartments on the upper floors and shops on the porch level.

8210 Main Street: Say It In Stitches and the Masonic Lodge

Originally, a two-story frame building was located here. In fact, Christian Eckert (see above) made ice cream here. He later demolished the frame structure to build the addition to the Howard House in the late 1800s. The three-story stone and brick addition was built in the Italianate style with scrolled brackets under the eves. After its use as the hotel addition, the building eventually hosted a variety of stores on the street level, including Paul's Market, Brown's Market, and Feaga's Market. Before Prohibition (1920-1933), a bar was located here. The building has also been used as a pool hall and barber shop.

Corner of Main Street and Church Road: Fire Station Museum

Please see Church Road on page 75 for information about this structure.

In the 1920s Scott Starr built this brick building for his undertaking business. It was later altered and housed apartments. Note the new, modern hearse.

8290 Main Street: Rock Hill Liquors
8294 Main Street: Ellicott Mills Art Gallery

This was part of a ten-acre parcel that was owned in 1819 by Irvin McLaughlin, then David Sprecher and E. A. Talbott. In 1887 there was a two-story frame structure on the site that was used as a print shop. In 1919 Scott Starr purchased the building for use as a funeral home. A new brick addition was added, and the frame structure was renovated. The building was also known as Starr apartments.

8298 Main Street: Private resident
8304 Main Street: Suitable Shirts

This building, or some part of it, was probably used in the early 1800s as a tavern and/or hotel. The original owner experienced many financial problems, but eventually his widow made a success of his venture. The story began when Irvin McLaughlin purchased ten acres of Mount Misery (a land patent that included this property) from Elias, William, and Thomas Brown in 1819 for $500 an acre. He was to pay $100 down, $400 within four months, and the balance in three equal payments. In 1824 McLaughlin borrowed money from the Ellicotts. The mortgage on the property listed a vast amount of personal property indicating that McLaughlin did have a tavern or hotel on the site. The inventory included eight mahogany tables valued at $98; fifteen beds with bedding, sheets, blankets, listed for $275; five chamber looking glasses listed for $14; carpets; china; curtains; silver, including eight dozen wine glasses valued at $13; four horses, and a cow. The total value – $1,419. McLaughlin failed to make his payments to the Browns and subsequently conveyed the property to others, dying insolvent with many debts.

When the property was auctioned in 1826, the Browns purchased it again. They paid $6,250. They then sold the ten acres that included the tavern house, store house, stables, outhouses, all stock, furniture, Negroes, and animals to William Lorman. Deborah McLaughlin, widow of Irvin, married Edward Disney on July 21, 1835 in Baltimore City. Five years later she bought the property from Lorman for $6,000 – the same ten acres that her first husband had purchased in 1819. Mrs. Disney must have run a profitable business. A Martenet map of the 1860s referred to the site as Mrs. Disney's Union Hotel. It was also referred to as Mrs. Disney's Tavern. An 1870 newspaper, *Common Sense*, stated that Groves' City Hotel was at this location. However, a year later another newspaper recorded that D. Sprecher operated a store that sold dry goods, notions, hardware, and groceries in the brick building that was formerly known as the Union Hotel. By 1887 both the east and west sides of the building were used as dwellings. More recently a fabric shop operated on the west side.

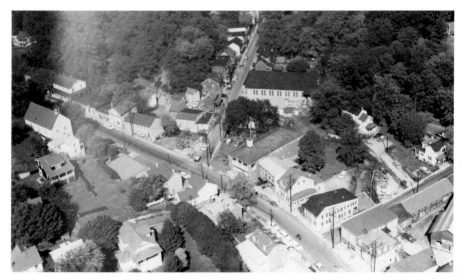

In this photograph from the early 1970s, Fells Lane intersected Main Street at the fire station (mid-center). Today all the houses on Fells Lane and to the left along Main Street are gone to make way for Ellicott Mills Drive and the parking lot behind the fire station.

8308 Main Street: Talbott Lumber Company

Originally two older buildings, one a dwelling and the other a grocery, stood at this location. E. Alexander Talbott and his father Edward A. Talbott purchased the property in 1885 from David Sprecher. They tore down the old structures to construct the present granite and brick two-story building, according to Celia Holland in *Ellicott City, Mill Town, USA.* The Talbotts were well known in the town. Evidently their lumber business was started by R. Gambrill about 1850. Holland recounts that the Talbotts suffered great losses in the floods of the 1860s when their business was located near the river. In 1870 Edward A. Talbott advertised as a dealer in building materials. The yard was located opposite the City Hotel (8304 Main Street), and the office was under the Patapsco Hotel, near the B&O Railroad. At the same time, Talbott advertised his agricultural store as carrying fertilizers, plows, garden seeds, and implements at the Town Hall. Families recalled that the Talbotts used four pairs of fine horses to make deliveries. When the roads were improved and paved, customers moved farther from town, and the Talbotts discontinued making deliveries. The Talbott Lumber Company has been owned by Rosen and Mazer since 1945.

Architecturally, the building represents the classic turn-of-the-century commercial facade. Note the arched windows and doors, the continuous stone sills, and granite steps.

The old police station (8316 Main) is at the right in this photograph. A World War II-era parade marches past the stores and dwellings to the west of the old station.

8316 Main Street: Storage

This building, constructed in the 1920s, was used as a garage. Around 1924 the Ellicott City commissioners bought the building for the county's second fire house, as a larger space was needed to accommodate "Big Kate," the American LaFrance triple combination 600-gallon-per-minute pumper that the county commissioners had proudly purchased in 1923. The second floor was converted to a six-room apartment for B. H. Shipley, Sr. and his family. Shipley had been hired by the commissioners to manage the fire company. He was a skilled mechanic who worked at the Green Cross Garage. His son, B. Harrison Shipley Jr., continues a life-long interest and devotion to the fire department. The building has also been used for the police station and the community action council.

8320 Main Street: Storage

This property was part of McLaughlin's ten acres, called "Mount Misery" (see 8298 Main Street). By 1860, Martenet's Map showed a structure here. The third story is probably a later addition. Through the years the building has been used for residences and offices: a residence for W. McClary, in 1860; a dwelling in 1887; an office for Dr. Leon Kochman; an office and residence for Dr. Miller; and an office for Harold Jones, a contractor.

8332 Main Street: Corner Clothes Closet

An 1839 plat indicates a store at this location. However, since Howard County had not yet been formed and there was no courthouse, the road up the hill had not been built. In 1860 Wesley Forrest occupied the property, and it was again listed with a dwelling in 1887. By 1895 Richard Feigley had established a business in this location. He then sold it to E. P. Ellis who later sold to Edward Pickett. Holzweig operated the United Food Store beginning in 1926, and his family lived above the store. He was also a charter member of the Ellicott City Kiwanis Club.

8344 Main Street: Nationwide Insurance
9398 Court Avenue: American Military Antiques

This is a two-part structure. The older section appears to be the east or brick portion. It was part of the ten acres called Mount Misery (see 8298 Main Street) during the mid-19th century. The brick house on the corner may have been Mrs. Disney's office. In 1843 she was assessed for a new brick office on the Pike (Main Street) valued at $200. She had the Union Hotel, one-half block east (see 8298 Main Street). The frame addition appeared by 1878; it was used as a residence and a sewing machine store.

8358 Main Street: Private residence

This frame house with its stone foundation was built by John Day as his residence and store in the 1870s. By 1887 the parcel was up for public auction. Clara Kraft became the owner in 1888. The building was also used for Dr. Gambrill's office and residence in the early 20th century. To the rear of the building was the stable for horse and buggy, now gone.

8370-8380 Main Street: Dr. Boman, DDS

Although altered through the years, the house was probably built in the 1840s. Jonathan Ellicott leased the property in 1839 to Jacob Timanus for $43 a year. The lease was reassigned to a Mr. Fort in 1840 and to John Day in 1849. The house appears to have been Day's store and home before he built the house at No. 8358 next door. After the flood of 1868, the property was sold to Dr. T. B. Owings for $2,600. The doctor survived the flood, but unfortunately his wife and six of his children drowned. His house stood adjacent to the river on the Baltimore County side. His wife, Margaretha, was 36, and the children were Mary Augusta and Maggie, 10; Kate, 8; Willie, 5; Thomas, 2; and Harry, 7 months. The family's "colored" servants, William and Louisa, were also lost, as well as the nursegirl, Martha. In 1871 Dr. Owings married Miss Nellie Polk of Sykesville. Later dentists included Drs. J. E. Shreve, Louis Brown, and George Hansen. William Bishop, DDS, maintained his practice here for many years until 1989.

8390 Main Street: Fire Station No. 2 (Lot 52 on the 1836 partition of Ellicott property)

As early as 1860, a blacksmith shop operated at this location. A double frame house built by George Ellicott in 1836 was located on the property to the west (Lot 53). The property then had a succession of owners: Robert Wilson, Josiah Groves, and Eli Hamilton. In 1872 Charles Makinson bought the property and operated a carriage factory and later, a blacksmith shop. By 1894 these frame buildings (which burned in 1913) were used as a dwelling and a grocery. The lot was purchased in 1937 for $2,500 for construction of a new fire house. The brick two-story fire station was completed by April 1939, at a cost of $33,684. The Public Works Administration paid 45 percent of the cost, and the county commissioners paid the balance, according to Shipley's *History of the Fire Department*.

Corner of Main Street and Ellicott Mills Drive

This simple two-story granite structure with a gable roof was built in the early 1800s. The building was preserved because it was used for court purposes in 1840-43 while the county's courthouse was built.

The original jail was in the cellar of a house that stood near the Courthouse; it was a damp cellar room, about 18 feet by 14 feet. In March 1850 the grand jury reported on the deplorable condition of this jail and declared it to be a nuisance and a revolting spectacle. A very narrow winding flight of steps was its only entrance. The steps were unsafe and shattered. During the grand jury's visit, the jail held six prisoners, two charged with murder. All prisoners – black and white, male and female – were crowded together in this cell. There were no beds, blankets, or sewer facilities. Within a short time, a new jail was built near the new courthouse on the hill. That jail facility is still standing as a part of the 1878 jail. Note how low the former courthouse building sits; this is the former level of the road and the original properties.

Log Cabin

This log cabin was originally located on Merryman Street, once called Missionary Lane. It was carefully dismantled, log by log, in the 1970s and reconstructed at its present location.

St. Luke's A.M.E. Church, located directly across Main Street from the restored cabin, had its beginnings in the vicinity of the original location of the cabin on Merryman Street. In 1890 the congregation laid the cornerstone for the new church. Following a custom that continues to this day, the congregation marched to the new building from the old church for the dedication ceremony.

The restored log cabin was reconstructed from a cabin originally located on Merryman Street. Pictured above is the log cabin at its original site

Main Street,
South Side

The south side of lower Main Street had small wooden frame stores in the early 20th century. The B&O station on the left had a covered stairway on the outside of the building for passengers going to Main Street. Note the billboard-style advertising on the Clark & Owings store.

8049 Main Street: Phoenix Restaurant and Casey's Antiques (Part of Lot 4 from the 1834 lottery)

This site was an empty lot as late as 1850 when it was part of Howard Swain's yard where he sold lumber, lime, and coal. He used the railroad depot as his office. The land had been purchased in 1850 for Hester Ann Rogers Putney, who then leased it out for $60 a year. From 1858 to 1887 the Bernard Fort family owned the property. According to 1887 records, a one-story grocery store stood on this corner. A second floor was added to the building about 1925. Other businesses located here included bars and restaurants operated by John O'Brian, Fissell, and Valmas.

8055 Main Street: Discoveries

This site was probably part of the Fort property when William Fort advertised in 1840 that he was located nearly opposite Brown's Hotel. If you were setting up housekeeping or burying a family member, you visited Mr. Fort, cabinetmaker and undertaker. His furniture included bedsteads, bureaus, tables, wardrobes, chairs, and pictures. Coffins made of poplar, walnut or mahogany, were lined with cambric, flannel, florence, or satin. He also advertised that he would accept sawn logs, planks, and scantling in poplar, walnut, buttonwood, cherry, or maple in exchange for furniture. Fort's son, Bernard, carried on the family business. Other businesses here through the years have included a furniture store in 1887, Kramer's Bar, Sanitary Grocery, France's Market, and more recently, Dorn's Grocery.

8057 Main Street: Alice's Country Cottage

The Easton family bought Fort's undertaking business in the 1880s. The Easton Funeral Home was located here until the late 1950s. The present building, built in the 1930s, replaced an early frame funeral home.

8059 Main Street: Empty lot

Fires are always a problem in urban areas and Ellicott City was no exception. A warehouse, the first known building at this location in 1887, was also the site of Clark's hardware store, opened about 1922. Also in the 1920s Ed Rodey operated the Earle Theatre here, but a 1941 fire destroyed the building and Roy's Cafe. The buildings were rebuilt and occupied by a billiards hall, a coin-operated laundry, and the office of Dr. Shpritz. In 1965 a fire broke out in the billiards hall and the businesses were destroyed. All that remains is an empty lot.

8069 Main Street: Great Panes (Part of Lot 10 in the 1830 Ellicott partition)

This three-story brick and stone building, covered with stucco, was probably built in the 1860s. According to old records, Thomas McCrea owned the property in 1860 and sold it in 1866 to James Curran. By 1887 sewing machines and notions were sold here, and later the building was known as the Goldberg Store. During the renovation of the Caplan

The Earle Theater, built in the 1920s, stood here until destroyed by fire in 1941, as was Roy's Cafe next door. Although rebuilt, the buildings burned again in 1965; all that now remains is an empty lot.

Department Store in 1925, the Caplans temporarily housed their business here. The building has also held Jones General Store, a pool hall and bar, Coroneo's confectionary and lunch, and the Patapsco Bicycle Shop. The stucco was added after the flood of 1972.

8081 Main Street: Source Unlimited (Part of Lot 10 in the 1830 Ellicott partition)

Samuel Ellicott leased this land in 1833 to Richard Partington, who built the granite stone house. Selman and Crooks, Baltimore merchants, bought the building in 1839 for $1500. The owner in 1849 was Collier who sold stoves, ranges, and tinware. Dorothy Kraft purchased the building in 1881 for Kraft's Meat Market. At the time of her death in 1916, a local newspaper speculated that Dorothy Kraft was the richest woman in Howard County. Note that this building is one of the few early stone houses with an unaltered exterior. The house has a gable roof, four bays, and the original stone entry threshhold.

8085 Main Street: Larry Beverunge, Contractor

A two-story frame dwelling was listed at this site in 1887. By 1894 a grocery store was located here. In the 1920s, Sam Curran built the new brick building for his tavern. Later it became Fisher's barbershop. In the 1930s, the Valmas brothers had a restaurant in the building. Bessie and Russell Moxley recall the "good old days" when you could enjoy a hamburger, drink, and sundae at Valmas for only 25 cents.

8089 Main Street: Baxter's Restaurant (Lot 133 in the partition of the George Ellicott property in 1839)

In 1860 S. Stark operated a store at this location. According to the 1887 records, the building was a two-story grocery. In 1894 the store became a fish market, and during the 1930s it was part of the Valmas Restaurant (see above).

8095 Main Street: Undergoing restoration
8101 Main Street: Renaissance Books
8103 Main Street: Nature Nook (Lots 130-132 on 1839 partition)

An 1830s frame stable converted into a dwelling was the earliest structure on this site. The original building is visible in the basement of 8103 Main Street. After its early residential use, the property has generally been used for commercial purposes. In the 1860s, if you needed hats, caps, boots, shoes, dry goods and millinery, you visited the Clothing Hall of H. Henke. He advertised in the local papers in 1868. By 1887 the following businesses were listed

The frame building at far left, once used as a tin shop, was torn down to build 8085-89. Rosenstock had not yet remodeled the front of his department store (8095-8103). Barely visible, a sign at the Caplan store reads, "We give S&H stamps". The North side of Main Street has changed little from this early 20th century photograph.

here: a two-story grocery, a three-story jewelry shop, and a boot and shoe shop. The buildings were purchased in 1918 by Hyman Rosenstock. In the late 1920s Rosenstock remodeled and combined them into a single, stuccoed-front building, where he operated a department store in competition with the Caplan Department Store.

8113 Main Street: East side (Lot 129 on 1839 Ellicott plat)

Although this building has been greatly modified over the years, it originally was of frame construction. A grocery store was at this location in 1887, followed by Brian's Grocery. During the 1940s the building also served as a library operated by the Howard County Women's Club.

8113 Main Street: West side – Act I and II Dress Shop (Lot 128 on 1839 Ellicott plat)

This building, like the one above, was constructed of log beams and covered with a wooden frame. It is known that there was a frame house on the property in 1836. In the 1850s Elizabeth Ellicott Lea inherited the property from her grandmother. Anthony Laumann purchased the property in 1860 for $650, and it stayed in the family until 1952. Laumann was said to have opened a barbershop in town in 1828, and records show the building was still in use as a barbershop in 1887. Phil Laumann continued the barbershop business, until Joe Miller took over. Old-timers recall that Laumann's shop had a sign that read "Cupping and Leeching", which indicates that in those days, barbers often drew blood for medicinal reasons. In more recent times, a wig store was located here.

8125 Main Street: Caplan's Antiques (Lots No. 127 and 143 on 1839 partition)

Picture this lot as it must have appeared in 1836. On the east side, Mary Stimmer had a frame house. David Jones owned the west half of the lot, where he had built a stone house in the 1830s (see 8129 Main Street). By 1887 one building was used as a dry goods store and the other as a grocery. The Caplan family came to town in 1895 and bought out Sol Davis' dry goods business. The Davises' son, Meyer, was a renowned orchestra leader in New York City during the 1920s. He returned to Ellicott City in 1972 to play for the Bicentennial Ball. The Caplans had the two buildings demolished in 1926 and built a new store. It was called Ellicott City's Daylight Department Store because of its large modern windows and skylights. The general contractor was William F. Thompson. The Caplan Department Store carried better merchandise for the "carriage trade" of Ellicott City.

Long-time businessman Sam Caplan, unofficial mayor of Ellicott City and well-known local citizen, passed away in early 1990 at the age of 90.

8129 Main Street: Stillridge Herb Shop (Part of Lot 9 on 1830 partition and part of Lot 143 on the 1839 Ellicott plat)

David Jones had a stone house on the lot as early as 1836; he was a baker, and the story is told that he enjoyed his drink. One day when Jones took the wagon to deliver bakery goods, he did not return. His wife, Sarah, looked out the shop window and recognized David's wagon going by, with a stranger driving it. She chased the wagon and questioned the driver. He informed her that he was an organ grinder, and that David had traded the wagon for his organ and monkey. What happened after that is not known. After David died, Sarah advertised three properties for sale in 1850. One building was rented to Isaac Strawbridge for $8 per month; the second, with an attached bake house, was occupied by Robert Lilly. The present stone building is probably half of David Jones' property. In recent years it held Kirkwood's Shoe Store and the Cavey brothers' barbershop.

8133 Main Street: Annie's (Part of George Ellicott's lot in 1836)

This lot and the one next door at 8137 Main Street were left to George Ellicott, Jr. by his father in 1832 and deeded to him by his mother Elizabeth in 1834. The younger Ellicott built a double stone house here, thus fulfilling his father's request that he build a residence on the lot. The building was purchased by Joseph Merkle in 1860 for $800. In 1887 the east side of the property was used by a carpet weaver on the east side, and a residence was on the west side. It is possible that the present stone building is part of Ellicott's old stone house. In recent years this building has been used for Fissell's Grocery and a Chinese laundry.

8137 Main Street: Commercial and Farmers Bank (Part of George Ellicott's property mentioned above)

The Washington Trust Company of Maryland bought the property in 1905 and erected the present three-story building. The Yates family had their grocery store in this location before the new bank was built. The bank was reorganized in 1935 as the Commercial and Farmers Bank.

This photograph, taken in the early 1900s, shows the new Washington Trust Bank building (now Commercial and Farmers Bank) flanked by two old store buildings: Fissell's Grocery and the New Store, run by John U. Brian. The New Store burned down in 1984. Fissell's was a portion of George Ellicott's property, possibly built in the 1830s.

Anita Cushing recalls that Mr. and Mrs. Norman Betts worked at the town's two banks. Whenever Mr. Betts, at Commercial and Farmers Bank, inadvertently received correspondence for the Patapsco Bank across the street, he would telephone Mrs. Betts and the two would meet at mid-point in Main Street and exchange errant business papers.

8141 Main Street through 8167 Main Street: Celebrate Maryland, Leidig's Bakery, Tusker's Gifts, Chateau Wine Supply, and Ellicott Square housing The Iron Rail, Just Arrived, Paper Doll, Quilt Studio, Ross Barber Shop, Ovella's Gifts, and Only the Best restaurant

These are new brick buildings, designed to fit into the street's older architectural style. After a fire in 1984 seriously damaged the previous buildings, they were torn down.

HISTORY OF BUSINESSES BEFORE THE 1984 FIRE:

8145 Main Street: Part of Lot 9 on Ellicott partition

In 1830 James Martin had a stone house here, and by 1887 there was a three-story boot and shoe shop. Other uses included John U. Brian's New Store, Hope & Wise Hardware, Peddicord Hardware & Appliances, and lastly, Chez Fernand.

8149 Main Street: Lot 126 on Ellicott partition

In 1836 Margery B. Anderson occupied a brick house for a yearly fee of $56. By 1887 a two-story grocery store was at this location; it was remodeled by Holzweig after 1932. Other businesses included Austin's, Olin's Five and Dime Store, and Leidig's Bakery.

8155 Main Street: Part of Lot 125 in 1839 but with no structure

A three-story general store was located here by 1887; it was followed by Blanks Clothing Store, Yates Record Shop, and The Antique Clock Shop.

8167 Main Street: Part of Lot 125 in 1839

A two-story drugstore was here in 1887. Other uses included Taylor's jewelry and music store, Gendason's dry goods, Olin's, and Marino's Frame and Art Shop.

8167 Main Street: Lot 124 in 1836

In 1836 Mary Myers leased a frame house for $32.66 a year. In 1849 the property was transferred to Ezekial Mills, and the house was assessed at $600. By 1887 the building housed a two-story tailor's shop. Other businesses included Loughran's Bakery, the editorial offices of the *Times*, and the Marino Gallery.

8169 Main Street: Lot 123 in 1836

Joshua Cross had a frame house here that was occupied by James Lea. By 1887 there was a two-story bakery in the building. Other stores were Sach's Economy Store, Johnson's Pharmacy, and The Iron Rail.

The 1860 Martenet Map showed a row of very early shops located on the above lots. They included I. J. Martin, Apothocary; J. Gaw; Kinzey store; B. Helm Shoe Store; J. McCrea store; and Rommell Taylor.

HISTORY OF STORES FROM 8173 MAIN STREET TO 8191 MAIN STREET

In 1836 this end of the block included a stone house leased to Norfolk for $44 a year; a lot leased to Gaw for $45 a year; a stone house on Lot 120 belonging to I. Mercer; and Lots 118 and 119 – all part of Lot 8 from the 1830 partition of Ellicott property. Nearly 30 years later, in 1860 the properties at this end of the block included D. Gallo, barber; B. Preacher, tailor; and the post office, with N. C. Brooks as the postmaster. These same sites in 1887 housed a bakery, dry goods shop, grocery, general store, carpet weaver, and a residence.

Fire decimated this strip of stores in 1915. The blaze appeared to have started at Marshall Bacon's Grocery (now No. 8173) and destroyed five buildings, including the post office. Edward A. Rodey,

Before the 1984 fire these five buildings stood between the bank and "Pickwick Papers." From left to right are Chez Fernand, Leidig's Bakery, The Antique Clock Shop, Marino's Frame and Art Shop, Marino Gallery, and The Iron Rail.

postmaster, and his postal workers saved the mail and other valuable papers. In the spring of 1915, four new brick structures at 8173-8191, one known as the Butke Building and another known as the Wallenhorst Building, replaced the burned-out buildings.

8173 Main Street: Sheppard Art Gallery

C&P Telephone Company used the building for twenty years; it was then occupied by The Pickwick Papers Company.

8181 Main Street: Kids At Heart

Stores here have been American Stores, Crook's Grocery, and the Patapsco Pharmacy.

8185 Main Street: Groomes Jewelry

Businesses at this location have included a post office, Read's Drug Store, Caplan Shoes, Gil's Lunch, and Dee's Kitchen.

8191 Main Street: Maryland Country Sampler

One of the first businesses was Wallenhorst Haberdashery. An A&P store and Dr. Shpritz's office were also at this location.

8197 Main Street: Taylor Furniture Store

After the 1915 fire, the corner of Main Street and Columbia Pike was unoccupied. Isaac Taylor's son, Irving, remembered making mudpies there as a young child. When Isaac decided to build the new building in 1924, he received a commitment of a loan "on a handshake" from a local bank. After plans were finalized with Julius Kinlein, the contractor, Isaac requested the funds only to find that the bank had withdrawn its promise. Fortunately his mother-in-law, Rachel Caplan, was a successful businesswoman, and she contacted a Baltimore bank that provided the necessary financing.

This was Isaac's fourth location. He expanded as his business grew from jewelry and optometry to music boxes, and then to home appliances. In the mid-1920s Isaac sold appliances door-to-door. Even before there was rural electricity, early appliances used motors, powered by generators, to ease the

At the intersection of Columbia Pike and Main Street, the signpost clearly shows Routes 29 and 40. This gas station was removed when the Pike was widened. Main Street was U.S. 40 before World War II and into the 1940s. This photograph was taken during the 1940s.

load of housework. During the Depression, families continued payments on appliances, sometimes as little as five cents at a time.

Active in the community, Isaac Taylor was appointed to the school board where he worked at improving the school system.

Although the business today carries the family name, the Taylors sold out over 40 years ago. Irving Taylor was affiliated with the Taylor Manor Hospital on College Road, which the family had purchased in 1939. After Isaac Taylor sold the store, he assisted with the administration of the hospital.

Intersection of Main Street and Columbia Pike

Columbia Pike is much wider today than when it was first used as a road. If you looked west from the intersection in 1836, you would see seven lots between the Pike and Hamilton Street, before the post office. However, only two frame houses were built on that western portion. In the late 1890s a large frame grocery store operated by James Steward stood proudly where the west half of the Pike is today.

The Ellicott Theater was built after a fire on April 5, 1940 destroyed Berger's Grocery (Peoples Stores) and Der Wong's Laundry, adjacent to the Church of God.

With the advent of the automobile, the store was demolished for the construction of a Standard Oil gas station. In this era the Pike was Route 29, and Main Street was U.S. Route 40. As traffic increased, the station was removed to widen the road.

8225 Main Street: Onstage Productions and The Little Theatre on the Corner

In 1887 B. Mellor operated a carriage factory on Main Street, and there was a blacksmith and woodwork shop at the rear of the building. A men's furnishings store was located on the west side. Later Berger's Grocery and Der Wong's Chinese laundry were at this location. These frame buildings were all destroyed by fire in 1940.

The Ellicott Theater (present building) was built by Isaac Taylor in 1940. The building has also housed Eddie's Cut Rate Store.

8227 Main Street: Southern Methodist Church

In 1860 Shane had a harness shop here. Mayfield bought the shop in 1865, but he had to agree to not build a stable on the lot. Mayfield was still operating his shop in 1887. In 1933 the Church of God bought the property for use as a church.

8231 Main Street: Antique Clock and Watch Shop, Main Street Comics (Lot 23 and part of Lot 22 from 1839 plat)

In 1864 the lot was purchased for $190 by Thomas Isaacs, and by 1887 a hardware store was located here. Stigler's Bakery operated in this location in the early 1900s. The structure was rebuilt in the 1920s as Higinbothom's Funeral Home.

8239 Main Street: Rebel Trading Post (Lot 21 and part of Lot 22, 1839 plat)

Zedikiah Isaacs was an early owner of the property, which he sold for $315. By 1887 the site housed a bakery. After Charles Buetefisch, a tailor, bought the property in 1897, he remodeled the store several times. Buetefisch inherited his business; his father, Henry Christian Buetefisch, had opened a tailor shop in town about 1870, three years before Charles' birth. Henry's store was located east of the Pike; however, Charles had a more important location than his father's. His shop and dwelling were directly across the street from the early fire station. Whenever fires were reported to him, he ran across Main Street and rang the fire bell to alert other volunteers.

As a tailor Charles bought local wool and raw furs, such as muskrat, opossum, racoon, and mink. After his death, Charles' widow sold the shop but retained the right to occupy the second floor apartment during her lifetime.

Other businesses have included Etta's Beauty Shop, Lane's Modern Cleaners and Dryers, Crystal Restaurant, and DeHaven's Milk Bar.

8241 Main Street: Fringes Dolls and Sweet Rememberings Doll Hospital (Lot 20 on 1839 plat)

This lot was sold in 1899 for $580. Stigler bought the property for a plumbing business in 1901 for $825. Bounds Law Firm also had an office here.

8247 Main Street: Yates Hardware and Grocery

According to an 1836 plat, John Day had a new frame house built on the corner. That house was sold in 1863 to Margaret Hughes Poland, who sold it in 1867 to Michael and Mary McGilligan for $1400. When Michael died, Mary married Charles Powers. He later died, and she continued living in the house until her death. Bladen Yates remembers that the old house stood below

This row of buildings was torn down to construct the post office. The Hillsinger Funeral Home and Gaither Livery Stable were located here.

street level. The structure was demolished in 1925 for the Yates' grocery store; however, a stone foundation of the old house remains. The two-story dwelling on the east side of the Day house was Jane Scott's house. In 1858 Scott leased her property to Ann Tonge for $20 a year. Bladen Yates' grandfather moved his business from the site of the Washington Trust Bank in 1905 to this building. Their Model T delivery truck brought groceries directly to the housewife's door, a true luxury. After his grandfather built the new grocery store on the corner (the old Day house site), Mr. Yates opened a hardware store.

The 1860 Martenet map indicates that three attorneys occupied offices in this row: J. R. Clark, E. W. Sands, and G. B. Dorsey. In addition, there were other businesses in the row of buildings: Shane's harness shop, Mrs. Hudson's shop, and Mr. Norris' business.

8267 Main Street to 8293 Main Street (between Hamilton and Forrest Streets): Post Office, Reedy Electric, Crossroad Design, and Christmas Company. Tersiguel's French Restaurant is scheduled to open here in September by the former owners of Chez Fernand.

None of the original buildings at this location remain, but imagine the scene in 1839. Hamilton had a stone and wood house (Lot 139); Treakle had a frame house; and John Forrest also had a stone house. There were three vacant lots along Main Street and sixteen lots platted to the rear of these lots, where today's parking lot now stands.

By 1850 Forrest advertised that he stocked dry goods, groceries, Queensware, and hardware. That same year Dr. S. S. Sykes, a dentist, advertised that his residence was two doors from J. Forrest's store. Sykes publicized that he attended to diseases of teeth and gums, extracted teeth with the least possible pain, and plugged teeth with gold or silver foil.

By 1887 there were four dwellings, two dentists, one undertaker, and a warehouse. J. Gaither operated a livery stable and a delivery business at the rear of these properties. The back of the property also contained at least four dwellings on a driveway circling the livery area.

Of the present buildings in this block, No. 8293 is the oldest. It was built in the 1890s by Mordecai Gist Sykes as his new home and dental office. Sykes is remembered as riding his high bicycle every two weeks to his office at the Springfield State Hospital in Sykesville. He was a prominent businessman and once served as the mayor. Later, state and county offices used the building.

A young Mordecai Gist Sykes poses for the photographer. Following the profession of his father, he became a dentist and opened a practice in Ellicott City. Dr. M. G. Sykes built the large white house on Main Street, adjacent to Hamilton Street, where his family lived and he practiced dentistry. Dr. Sykes was Mayor of Ellicott City for two terms, from 1889 to 1897.

The Reedy Building was constructed in 1924 and used as the Ellicott City Garage, a Ford agency.

The new post office was dedicated on December 7, 1940. Five or six frame buildings were demolished to make way for the postal building. Note how the simple stone structure fits in with the other Quaker-style buildings in town.

8307 Main Street: First American Management, "Shops at Ellicotts Mills" and P. J.'s Restaurant (Lot 70, vacant, on Ellicott plat in 1836)

In 1878 this lot contained the lumberyard for Edward A. Talbott, which was later moved across the street. Several frame houses were built in the early 1900s; they have since been demolished.

Miller Chevrolet, at their new location (8307 Main Street), collected tires for the war effort during World War II. The house next door was later torn down.

Charley Miller purchased the property in the 1930s and built a new showroom for his Chevrolet dealership. He already owned the Green Cross Garage, an early Chevrolet dealership operated by Melville Scott. The Scott garage was located in the large red frame building behind the post office. In those days, you could drive through from Hamilton Street to Columbia Pike. Miller later moved his dealership to U.S. Route 40.

In 1968 the building was sold to Stromberg Publishing Company, owner of *The Ellicott City Times* that later became *The Howard County Times*. In 1980 the *Times* was sold to the Patuxent Publishing Company in Columbia.

8321 Main Street: Copy Center and Terenzio Piano Studio

This building has been recently altered and enlarged. Before modifications, the building served as the street headquarters for the Bicentennial activities in 1972. A cleaning business has also been at this location.

The Green Cross Garage was located on Hamilton Street behind the post office. One could also enter from the Columbia Pike. Today the red buildings are used as storage for Taylor's Furniture Store.

8329-8333 Main Street: Craig L. Stewart, Architect

Recently restored by Craig Stewart, the building was built by Caleb Merryman in 1836. Note that the adjacent street is named after this same Merryman. According to the records, the building was occupied by H. Thorne during the 1860s and was mostly used as a residence. In recent years the building has hosted a variety of shops.

8341 Main Street to 8345 Main Street: Bridals and Fashions (Lot 73 with house on 1836 plat)

This structure was one of the early stone houses in Ellicotts Mills. However, it has been modified and added onto through the years. The lot was owned by William McLaughlin by 1839, and by J. H. Leishear in 1878. Leishear had lost his property near the river in the 1868 flood and subsequently moved up on Main Street.

According to Celia Holland in *Ellicott City, Mill Town USA,* Joe Leishear was a grocer from the "old school." He stocked items such as paper collars when men no longer used them, and he did not provide paper bags. He chose to wrap all purchases in paper instead. This building was Leishear's

The post office lobby contains large murals depicting local history. One wall holds a modern scene showing local landmarks; another shows the Ellicotts clearing and plowing the fields. The murals were painted by 21-year-old artist, Petro Paul De Anna.

residence; his store was located where the post office now stands. In the early 1930s, the front was added to the first floor to make room for a grocery. The recent renovations have uncovered attractive old features such as the stone fireplace and an arch at the bay window.

8357 Main Street: Robert Brown, Attorney (Lot 48 with structure on the 1839 plat, leased to Charles Timanus, stonemason)

This stone building was constructed in the early 1830s. As early as 1860 A. J. and George Isaac owned the property. A. J. Isaac owned the granite quarry on the B&O Railroad. He advertised that they furnished granite work for curbing, platforms, and sills; ashler (square stone) for bridges; and rubble for walls. By 1887 the building was divided into two separate dwellings with a kitchen to the east. Today, Robert Brown has restored the structure.

8385 Main Street: Judges's Bench (Part of land patent Mount Misery, owned by Thomas, Elias, and William Brown; sold by Browns to Irvin McLaughlin in 1819)

In 1853 Sophia Frost bought the property for $390, and it remained in the Frost family for over 100 years. Commercial users have included Joe Berger's Grocery and Bode Floors. The 2-1/2 story building was probably built before

1878 and has been altered through the years. The stone on the top two stories has been covered over.

8391 Main Street: Waddell and Reed, Gallery Greetings and Gifts (Part of Mount Misery)

This building appears in the records as early as 1887. For many years it was used as a residence, however Leonard Mear also had a confectionary store here.

8405 Main Street: Part of Fire Department property

Martin's blacksmith shop was once at this location. For a period of time, a movie theater for "colored" patrons was located above the blacksmith shop. The shop was torn down, and in the 1930s Charley Miller of Miller Chevrolet built a gas station. Dick Wall later had a garage here.

In 1958 Hollywood excitement came to Ellicott City with the filming of the movie, "The Goddess," a story written by Paddy Chayefsky based on the life of Marilyn Monroe and starring Kim Stanley, Lloyd Bridges, and Patty Duke. This photograph shows a scene being filmed on Main Street, with the Rosenstock building in the background.

Maryland Avenue

Trains pulled into the Ellicott City station regularly for many years. In this photograph, circa the early 1900s, the stationmaster has freight ready to be loaded while behind him, two ladies in long skirts and a man wait to board the train, eastbound to Baltimore. Also pictured is the Patapsco Hotel, with Angelo's Cottage on the hill behind the Hotel.

A GIFT OF LAND FOR THE RAILROAD

In the early 1800s George, Samuel, Andrew, and John Ellicott owned four lots that were between the river and Maryland Avenue. The lots were numbered 16 to 19 on the 1830 partition.

The brothers gave parts of Lots 16, 17, and 18, a total of 52,125 square feet, to the B&O Railroad. The deed read that the land would be used "as a place of deposit for said company." (From this use comes the term "depot" for train station.) According to the deed, the Ellicotts charged the B&O nothing for the property "due to the benefits to be derived from such a location." And indeed it was the railroad that put Ellicott City on the map.

After the station was built in 1830, Andrew Jackson became the first President to ride on a train. In 1833 he traveled by stagecoach to Ellicotts Mills and boarded the train for the trip to Baltimore.

By 1887 covered steps came down the side of the granite depot from the track level of the station to Main Street. At the turn of the 20th century, frame buildings were constructed along lower Main Street on the railroad property. These frame buildings, owned by the railroad, held businesses such as a "speak-easy," clothing store, barbershop, lunchroom, restaurant, and liquor store. When Maryland Avenue was widened, the buildings were torn down. Two wooden bridges crossed the Tiber River from Main Street to the depot yard.

B&O RAILROAD

This simple two-story granite building has the distinction of being the first and oldest commercial station in this country. Construction was completed in 1831 on the terminus for the first twelve miles of commercial track laid in the United States. The granite came from one of the local quarries. One end of the building was designed for engine and car repair, the center section was to accommodate freight and produce, and the other end housed the superintendent's office. Passengers used the Patapsco Hotel facilities to wait for their trains.

As steam engines became larger, the station building could no longer be used for engine service. In the mid-1800s the building was renovated to provide passenger waiting rooms. The station's turntable, built in the 1860s, was also abandoned after the B&O expanded. Engine repair and turn work was shifted to the yards in Baltimore. Only the turntable base and a few parts now remain, which was recently partially excavated. Passenger service was discontinued in the 1950s and freight service in the 1970s. Hurricane Agnes in 1972 put The Old Main Line of the B&O out of commission, and the tracks sat silent for many years before the Chessie System, now CSX, reopened them. Today this building houses the Ellicott City B&O Railroad Museum which has artifacts, a series of changing exhibits from the early days of the B&O operations, and a research library.

The smaller brick freight house was built in 1885. It now holds an operating HO gauge model railroad layout of the 19th century Patapsco Valley from Baltimore to Ellicott City. A "labor of love" by railroad enthusiasts, the scale replica recreates many of the areas and landmarks through the valley and into the town. An interesting multi-media sight and sound presentation tells the history of the early B&O railroad.

3720 Maryland Avenue: Clark's Antiques Depot (Lot 4 from the 1833 lottery included an early tavern stable — see Lottery section under "Main Street, North Side")

In 1860 Howard Swain operated a business selling lumber, lime, and coal near this location. He had his office at the railroad building. J. W. Dorsey bought the site in the 1870s and built the present frame warehouse about 1885. He sold coal, hardware, fertilizer, and operated a farm supply business. His property was bounded by the Tiber River, the depot yard, St. Paul Street, and the property of Milton Easton. E. T. Clark bought Dorsey's store, warehouses, stables, and coal yard. There was a practical clause in the deed; it stipulated that seller William Dorsey could not operate a similar business within 20 miles of Ellicott City for ten years. In the early 20th century when Billy Owings was in partnership with Clark, the business operated as Clark and Owings. Clark moved to this building from Main Street around 1920. Clark's Hardware moved to a new location on U.S. Route 40 in the 1970s.

TIBER ALLEY

The Alley's cobblestones, laid between 1894 and 1899, remind one of similar roadways in Europe. Various businesses have operated in this picturesque setting. During a flood in the 1950s, John Valmas' automobile was washed away when one of the garages collapsed into the Tiber River.

8061 Tiber Alley: Wagon Wheel Antiques

Easton Undertakers used this building for a livery stable and equipment storage during the late 19th and early 20th centuries. An old horse-drawn carriage is still stored on the second floor.

8069 Tiber Alley: Sidestreets Restaurant

Although greatly changed through the years, this building was once a stone mill, typical of those built in the mid-1800s. According to records, Thomas McCrea purchased the property in 1850 from Nathaniel and Thomasine Ellicott of Chester County, Pennsylvania. McCrea advertised that same year that he sold pure buckwheat meal at his Depot Mill.

During McCrea's tenure at the mill, Eleanor Griffin sent her son there to master the trade. Thomas Griffin was indentured to McCrea to learn to be a blacksmith and miller. He was to serve from age 17 to 21 and receive schooling. In 1878 the building served as William Collier's flour mill. In the 1880s B. F. Hawes operated the Ellicott City Mills here and crossed the Tiber by a wooden bridge to get to Main Street.

Herman Shriver found a new use for the building in the 1890s. He formed a company to provide the first electric power and lights in the town, and sold stock to prominent local citizens, including Gaither, Sykes, Isaacs, Talbott, Yates, Oldfield, Kraft, and many others. The company operated from the stone grist mill, using water power and steam. Ezekial R. Moxley was the first operator, with assistants James Cavanaugh and James Mellor. According to Ezekial's son, Mark Moxley, the first lights were installed on Main Street, Fells Avenue, Church Road, St. Paul's Street, and New Cut Road to the swimming pool.

Between 1903 and 1905 the Patapsco Light and Power Company purchased the Ellicott City Plant and operated it until they were able to supply power from the Orange Grove Plant. Long disused, the old water wheel was washed away in the flash flood of 1953, according to Mark Moxley.

The original location of the Patapsco Bank, St. Paul Street at Maryland Avenue. The bank moved to Main Street in the 1880s. This stone building served as the parochial school for St. Paul's Church from the 1920s to the 1960s.

ST. PAUL STREET

The original Patapsco Bank, built in the 1830s, stands where Maryland Avenue meets St. Paul Street. The Bank moved to Main Street about 50 years later. The building later served the community as a parochial school for white students, started in 1922 by St. Paul's Church. Black students attended school in a frame building near the Rectory.

St. Paul's Roman Catholic Church is pictured with the buildings of Rock Hill College to the rear.

St. Paul's Catholic Church

The church was dedicated on December 13, 1838 and enlarged in 1859.

According to Celia Holland, the development of the National Pike and the construction of the railroad brought the Irish, German, and English Roman Catholic immigrants into the area. She recounts that George Ellicott Jr. married Barbara Agnes Peterson Iglehart, a Roman Catholic widow.

Before St. Paul's was constructed, Roman Catholics worshipped at Doughoregan Manor. When John Fahey arrived in 1822 he found just three other Catholics at the Mills, one of whom was John Joyce (Joice), a freedman from the Manor. After St. Paul's was built, the parsonage next door (west) was constructed in 1844.

In 1914 one of baseball's legendary players was married at the church. Babe Ruth (1895-1948) was just beginning his baseball career when he married Helen Woodford on October 17 in a small private ceremony here. This was Ruth's first marriage.

St. Paul's Street becomes either New Cut Road and leads south, or climbs the hill as College Avenue.

St. Peter's Episcopal Church stood to the rear of St. Paul's for nearly 100 years. The area is now a parking lot. When St. Peter's burned around 1939, it was rebuilt west of town on Rogers Avenue.

NEW CUT ROAD

The original pathway to the Quaker Meeting House was in the general direction down New Cut Road (see meeting house entry on Columbia Pike).

In the 1800s there was a row of old houses and log cabins along New Cut. In 1937 Tom Randall, an 80-year-old former slave, talked about his

One of two double log cabins built by George Ellicott, probably early 1800s. They stood on New Cut Road. In the early days the Quakers walked down a lane (later New Cut Road), crossed the stream and climbed the hill to the meeting house. The meeting house is now approached from Columbia Pike.

past in an interview. He recalled that he was born in a shack on New Cut Road in 1856. His mother was Julia Bacon, a cook at Howard House. She was allowed to take her young son with her to work. He remembered eating from the pots and pans after she had cooked fried chicken or game. As he grew older he helped carry wood, empty the garbage, and perform other chores to help her at Howard House.

Another tradition says that a particular bull often startled the residents of the cabins when he poked his head through their open windows and greeted them with a "mooo." The bull was part of a herd of cattle from nearby Rock Hill College (see below). The herd grazed on Forty Acres (see below), which was off New Cut Road.

College Avenue: Rock Hill College

Records show that Isaac Sams operated Sams' Academy for boys at this site as early as 1820. Sams feared the school would lose its access from the turnpike when the railroad started construction over his road. The courts required that the railroad provide a new road to the early academy, probably the same route used today.

The Christian Brothers, a Catholic order, purchased the property in 1857, renamed it Rock Hill, and continued to operate an academy here. During the Civil War the academy became an institute and after 1865, a college.

By 1890 Rock Hill College had grown from a small 1820s boy school into this large and impressive granite structure.

In 1850 five prominent citizens sent a letter to the newspaper praising Rock Hill Academy. "Feeling a deep interest, as we are sure you do, in the cause of education and in the success of the various schools located in our midst we cannot refrain from expressing our entire satisfaction at witnessing the late Examination at the Rock Hill Academy. The system of teaching, the progress made by the pupils and the manner in which they acquitted themselves, inspire us with great confidence in the abilities of Mr. Carter (the Principal) as an Instructor..."

Rock Hill College educated young men at the collegiate level for nearly 50 years, until it was destroyed by fire in 1923. Neighbors remember taking the young students into their homes so that the boys could continue their education by attending Calvert Hall in Baltimore.

Granite from the Rock Hill College was used to build the new Ellicott City High School in 1925.

In 1925 the new Ellicott City High School opened on the site of the burned college. Stone from the old college was used for the new school. Julius Kinlein, Sr. was the contractor.

The new school also included primary grades. A new Ellicott City High School on Montgomery Road was built in the late 1930s, and the building on College Avenue continued as an elementary school until the 1970s.

Burned and abandoned for many years, Ellicott City High School on College Avenue is now under renovation and will be used for residences.

Forty Acres

Rock Hill College included a large recreation area along New Cut Road, known as Forty Acres. Here the young men from the College played their ball games and swam in the local facilities. A nearby spring provided water for drinking. Starting in the 1920s primary schools throughout the county used to celebrate the arrival of Spring on "Field" or "Rally Day." The students came into Ellicott City and paraded through town to Forty Acres for their athletic competitions.

Later Sam Caplan purchased it and operated a day camp for Jewish boys. In the 1950s it was a public swimming pool where lessons were given by the Red Cross.

NOTE: It is not advisable to walk along College Avenue beyond the school because of traffic and lack of sidewalks. However, there are places of note beyond the old school property.

Lilburn

The large granite house with a four-story Romanesque tower is one of the county's finest architectural landmarks. Named Lilburn, the property was also known as "Hazeldene." It was built about 1857 by Henry Hazelhurst who operated the Baltimore Engineer Works. The plant manufactured machinery, including iron bridges and boilers. The house remained in the Hazelhurst family until 1900.

For a short time the Odd Fellows Lodge owned the property. The house burned in the 1920s when the Maginnis family lived there. The stone walls withstood the fire, and the family used timber from the property to rebuild the interior. During the 1930s a home for retarded children operated in the large twenty-room house.

Since the house resembles a stone castle, it has attracted its share of ghost stories, especially at Halloween. Owners like the Sherwood Baldersons experienced the presence of "spirits" during the years they lived in Lilburn, according to Celia Holland. One memorable experience involved a chandelier, mysteriously swinging without visible cause, during a dinner party.

Other College Avenue homes

Sitting back from the roadway is Maple Cliffe, built in the early 20th century by Samuel Radcliffe. Later Julius Kinlein, who was the contractor for the construction of the 1925 Ellicott City High School, moved here from Baltimore City. As a prominent contractor, he built a number of the homes along College Avenue for his five daughters and their families.

The White Duck Bed and Breakfast

This is a Victorian-style home where Dr. Keister, a local dentist, lived in the mid-1900s.

Taylor Manor Hospital

Early in the 20th century Dr. White operated the Patapsco Sanitarium on the outskirts of Ellicott City on College Avenue. In 1939 the Isaac Taylor family purchased the property and, for a short time, it was known as the Pinel Clinic in honor of a famous psychiatrist.

Taylor Manor Hospital as it appears today. Drawing courtesy of Taylor Manor Hospital.

The family later changed the name to Taylor Manor Hospital. The facility has been enlarged and specializes in psychiatric diagnosis, treatment, and education for adolescents and adults. Drs. Irving and Bruce Taylor, son and grandson respectively of Isaac Taylor, are principals in the operation of the hospital.

Church Road

In 1894 Church Street was called Ellicott Street. B. Mellor's Carriage Factory was located on the left side of the road opposite the Howard House; it is no longer standing. The Howard House and its addition, which both front on Main Street, also have access to Church Road.

The restored fire station in its unique location on the corner of Church Road and Main Street.

Fire Station

In the triangular lot between Main Street and Church Road is the town's first fire station, constructed in 1889. The bell in the cupola notified the volunteers of a fire. The first equipment was a ladder truck drawn by horse or man.

Initially a two-story structure was planned, but only $500 was raised, which paid for just a one-story building. The first fire equipment was a Howe Fire Engine, manufactured in Indianapolis. It was known as a

"Side-Stroke" hand-operated, horse-drawn piston pumper. There also was a two-wheel hose reel. The building has been restored to its original style to serve as a fire museum in the future.

Emory Methodist Church

The original Emory Methodist Church was completed in 1838, and was named for Bishop Emory. Construction cost was $6,181.34 plus $1,946 interest. When the church was built in 1838, Jake Timanus laid the stone, W. S. Harrison was the carpenter, and Jesse McKenzie was the plasterer. Lumber and materials came from W. E. Fells' lumberyard.

The town's YMCA in 1854 was granted permission for use, and in 1865 Captain McCreary's application to conduct a "day school" was approved. The Cadets of Temperance, who organized to control the use of alcohol, were allowed to use the basement at no charge. While the trustees regularly granted use for meetings related to moral or religious activities, political organizations were denied access.

A resolution was adopted in 1838 that decreed the use of tobacco be discontinued in the chapel. At that time women sat on the left, and men on the right with square wooden boxes filled with sand provided for the disposal of tobacco juice. In 1888 at its 50th anniversary, the church was considerably

Emory Methodist Church, completed in 1838, was remodeled 50 years later. Church trustees were responsible for deciding who could use the facility. In 1839 Primary School No. 45 rented the Sunday school room for four years at $60 a year. The "Ten Hour Association," a group striving to limit working hours at the mills to ten hours a day, and Miss Mary Thompson's select school were refused its use.

Dr. Martin's home on Church Road at Emory Street, built in the 1880s and recently restored. The gentleman in the foreground is unidentified.

remodeled at a cost of $3,500. Parishioners used the Presbyterian and Lutheran churches nearby while the building was being renovated. In the "new" church, seating was no longer segregated by sex. Stained-glass windows were added, and in 1892 electric lights were installed.

Large frame house on the corner

Dr. Isaac Martin, the well-known and prominent druggist, purchased the lot opposite the Methodist Church in 1872 and built a large frame house. In 1868 he advertised his Oriental Tooth Wash for cleaning and preserving the teeth, hardening the gums, sweetening the breath, imparting an agreeable taste to the mouth, and arresting the progress of decay by preventing the accumulation of tartar upon the teeth.

Dr. Martin also manufactured and sold an Elixir of Calisaya Bark for weak stomachs; family pills (entirely vegetable); and vermifuge, a "pleasant, safe and effectual remedy for worms in children."

Other houses of interest

In the 1860s and 1870s Miss Elizabeth W. Tilghman lived in the frame house on Church Road across Emory Street from Martin's house. She bought

The young black man is holding Dr. William Hodge's horse in front of his large, white frame Church Road home, which is not visible. In the background is the Presbyterian parsonage, now a private home known as the "Old Manse."

the property in 1858 for $850 and constructed a home, which has had many changes through the years.

The granite house adjacent to the Methodist Church belonged to Samuel Powell before 1860. He built an addition that was assessed in 1848 at $200. This was a considerable sum, since some new houses were assessed at this same value. By 1878 this was the home of Mrs. MacGill. Her two neighbors to the east were Dr. William Hodges and Lewis Watkins.

On Church Road, opposite from the residences of Mrs. Macgill and Dr. Hodge's and next to Miss Tilghman's home, is another granite home. It is the former Presbyterian parsonage, the "Old Manse," that was built in 1850. After a fire in 1939 the house was rebuilt. It is now a private residence.

The former Lutheran Church (the white frame building near the bend in Church Road) was founded in 1875 by a group of Ellicott City residents who had been worshipping in Catonsville. The German Lutheran population had increased over the years, and a separate church was now feasible. The original church was constructed for about $3,500, and the mortgage was burned in 1920. Later alterations were made to form a vestibule and extend the belfry. The adjacent parsonage was built between 1908 and 1912 for $2,500.

Early families in the church were Keiner, Kraft, Laumann, Herrman, Rody, Wehland, Werner, Gerwig, Wosch, Buetefisch, and Miller. Services were held in German. Soon after the church was constructed, its members approached the local school commissioners and requested a public school for German-speaking students. Although their request was not granted immediately, eventually classes for German-speaking children were conducted in the church's basement.

Angelo's Cottage (Castle Angelo)

This Gothic Revival structure was built by an architect, Alfred S. Waugh, around 1833. He is said to have named the house for his favorite artist, Michelangelo. In the 20th century the house was "modernized" and covered with brown shingles; however, the original house is thought to have been stuccoed. At one time steps led from the railroad to the cottage.

Church Road, continued

Church Road winds uphill for over a mile, and there are a number of landmarks to notice. On the hill above the road, then called Ellicott Street, was William Ellicott's home, built by 1830 (see Mount Ida on Court Avenue, page 86). Also called the "road to the Institute," the street led to the Patapsco Female Institute (see Court Avenue on page 86).

The romantic "Angelo's Cottage" is best viewed from the Patapsco River bridge, as the 1830s castle-like home overlooks the railroad and river. The architect who built it named it for the artist Michelangelo.

Past the Institute is the summer home where H. L. Mencken vacationed in 1888. Built circa 1870, it is called "The Vineyard." In his book *Happy Days*, Mencken fondly remembered the many experiences a city boy had in these "Rural Delights." He recalled Angelo's Cottage and the Institute on his trips to and from Main Street. Mencken also recalled visiting the Kraft's meat shop and the grocery to make purchases for his mother. Writing for the century edition of the *Times*, Mencken attributed his writing career to his exposure to the old printing presses at the *Times*, which was printed in the old stone building adjacent to the railroad tracks at that time. He had eagerly watched the printing operation as often as possible as a boy. Since he was so fascinated by the process, he had been given a toy printing set as a Christmas gift.

Linwood

At the end of Church Road stands a large stone house called Linwood. It was built before 1850. General Robert E. Lee visited at Linwood, where his daughter lived while she attended the Patapsco Female Institute. Once the

property of Major G. W. Peters, this sizable farm was owned into the 20th century by the Merrick family. Miss Mary Merrick was an internationally known Catholic laywoman with many honors from the Church and the Pope for her work with various charities. She founded the Christ Child Society, as well as several other charities, all operating today.

Linwood, circa 1950. Linwood served as a private home for over a century before it became a private school for special children. The large porch at the side was perfect for lazing away a summer afternoon in days gone by.

The building now houses Linwood School, a private facility that does outstanding work with autistic children. Its founder, Jeanne Simmons, has an impressive international reputation in this field.

According to Alice Ann Wetzel, an historic preservation planner for the county, the Linwood property was divided into lots in 1888, hence the homes on Church Road. Of the four houses originally built around 1888, three are still standing. A later home, built in the early 20th century, is a Sears Roebuck pre-fabricated house. It was shipped to Ellicott City by rail and hauled to Church Road by horse and wagon. The house was Model 120 and cost $1,278 to $1,660. This house is now listed in the National Registry of Historic Places. Today these early "pre-fab" homes, which reflect the values of the day, are particularly interesting to study.

Court Avenue

Before the construction of the courthouse in 1843, Court Avenue did not exist. Today, the road winds its way through an area once known as Mount Misery.

Originally an old path called Strawberry Lane brought children to and from the large stone and frame schoolhouse at the top of the hill. It ran north from Court Avenue to School Street. This schoolhouse held classes for elementary grades as well as the county's first high school students in the early 1900s. The building was razed after construction of the new school on College Avenue, and the stone and wood was then used to build houses on Columbia Pike.

The county's first high school stood near the courthouse at the end of Park Avenue, then called School Street. Elementary students attended here also; when enrollment grew, some classes were held in small separate buildings. Shortly after 1925 the school was torn down.

The 1843 courthouse remained unchanged for nearly 100 years.

Courthouse

Construction of the "commodious" courthouse began in 1841. The courthouse opened for the spring session in 1843, according to the *Howard District Press.* Although $20,000 was appropriated for the building, an additional $8,000 was required for completion.

At the original front (on Court Avenue) are two memorials, one to those who fought in the Confederate Army, and the other to veterans of World Wars I and II and the Korean War. The cannon on the lawn is said to have been captured at the Battle of Bladensburg during the War of 1812 by "Bachelor" John Dorsey. Dorsey, a brother of Judge Thomas Beale Dorsey of Mount Hebron, lived on St. John's Lane.

The courthouse is described as being Greek-inspired with some classical features. The architect was Samuel Harris, Charles Timanus the builder.

It is possible that young William Henry Hays worked on the construction of the new courthouse. Records show that on September 1, 1840, 19-year-old Hays was indentured to Timanus "to learn the art, trade and mystery of stone mason-stone cutter." William was to be permitted to attend night school.

His father would receive $50 the first year and $60 the next year in lieu of Timanus providing clothing, and the indenture was to end on April 9, 1843.

In 1938-39 a $40,000 addition, funded by the federal government, enlarged the original structure. During a recent multi-million dollar renovation, the building was enlarged and the interior was completely rebuilt. The entrance was also moved from its original front door to a grand new portico opening to the rear parking lot.

Lawyer's Row

The row of frame buildings opposite the courthouse has been called Lawyer's Row. The small building at 8351 Court Avenue on the corner opposite the church was the first office, built in the 1870s for Henry Wootton, a local attorney. By 1899 a small office was added to the east of Wootton's and another across from the courthouse.

Howard County Historical Society

Originally this building was the Presbyterian Church, and Court Avenue ended here. The first church at this site was completed about 1844; its congregation was formed from a church that had its beginnings at Thistle Mills, a cotton factory about two miles east of Ellicott City. Tragedy struck in 1894 after the congregation decided to enlarge the existing church. During construction, the building collapsed. An entirely new building had to be constructed at a cost of $10,000. The church bell was dedicated to the memory of E. A. Talbott, a local merchant and church member. When the congregation relocated outside of the city, Mrs. James Clark, Sr. purchased the property and presented it to the newly organized Howard County Historical Society. The building now houses a museum. The Society also owns the "schoolhouse" building to the rear of the church which is used as a research library. Incorporated into this much-altered structure is what may be the oldest building in Ellicott City, as it housed the Quaker School as early as 1790. Both the museum and the library are open to the public.

The young people were taught in the 1790s by Allen Wright, an outstanding teacher who welcomed any youngster who came to learn. According to the *Howard District Press* in 1847, there was also a more advanced school started later under the direction of Allen Wright's father, Joel. That school was held during the winter over the Ellicotts' store, and at the Friends Meeting House in the summer. Students came here when they advanced beyond Allen's schooling.

Oak Lawn Seminary

Incorporated into the courthouse renovation is a stone building with a wrought-iron porch. This structure was originally built in 1840 for the Edwin Parsons Hayden family. After Edwin Hayden's death, his family operated a private school, the Oaklawn Seminary for Girls, in the building in the 1850s. Later on attorney Henry Wootton made it his home.

At one time the Board of Education and the District Court used it for offices. Before the house was gutted for renovation, court employees told tales of smelling breakfast cooking when arriving for work in the morning, although the house had no kitchen. Turning doorknobs and creaking doors left some with little doubt that Hayden family spirits kept watch over their home.

Emory Street Jail (green cupola building to the rear of the courthouse)

The green cupola marks the location of the county's 1878 jail, reported as a "fine and commodious" structure at its completion. When the plans for the new jail were reported in the local newspaper in 1878, the cost of the structure was not to exceed $8,000. There were to be 16 cells, 8 feet by 10 feet, with iron-grated doors, and the interior would be whitewashed and heated by a large stove. The building was attached to the 1851 jail, which then became the warden's residence.

The 1878 jail served Howard County for over 100 years before the new detention center was built in Jessup. The building then housed Central Alarm and the Sheriff's Department. It is now used to hold prisoners during the day while awaiting a court appearance.

Standing in a grove of willow trees, Willow Grove, the 1878 jail, once presented a picturesque setting at the rear of the courthouse. Today, used to house prisoners on a temporary basis, it is called the Emory Street Jail.

Mount Ida

Mount Ida stands near the courthouse rear parking lot. The large, yellow stuccoed building was constructed by William Ellicott about 1830. Born on October 15, 1793 William was the sixth child of Jonathan and Sarah Ellicott. At age 40 he married Mary Elenora Norris and died three years later in 1836.

The structure then was the home of Judge John S. Tyson and his family for many years; later the Louis T. Clark family lived there. The Miller Land Company recently had the building stabilized and is now considering several options for its use.

The Patapsco Female Institute

The Institute is in ruins today, but imagine the scene as it was in 1837: a handsome, 57-room granite building with imposing columns, perched high on a hill overlooking Ellicott City and the surrounding countryside.

The school for young ladies was designed by Baltimore architect Robert Cary Long, Sr. and opened January 1, 1837 to teach "in a most thorough manner, every branch of Science, Literature and Taste, as well as of good morals and deportment constituting a solid accomplished education" (from Rev. J. H. Tyng, the first principal). Unfortunately for the Institute, the country was experiencing a recession in the late 1830s. Rev. Tyng wrote to

Mount Ida was a handsome home in the mid-19th century.

the president of the Board of Trustees that "the number of Boarders through the year [1837] has not averaged more than six..."

In 1841 Almira Hart Lincoln Phelps, a prominent educator, came to the school's rescue. She was engaged, along with her husband, to take charge. "I come to Maryland," she said, "in the full belief that an important and successful effect may now be made in this state for the promotion of female improvement..." The trustees gave her a lease for seven years. In lieu of rent, the Phelpses agreed to spend $200 a year to improve the buildings and premises. As part of this agreement, the interior of the building was remodeled to create comfortable apartments for the girls.

The following description of Almira Hart Lincoln Phelps is provided by Helen Mitchell of Howard Community College, who wrote her doctoral dissertation on Mrs. Phelps.

Mrs. Phelps brought an international reputation with her when she was named principal of the Institute. Her science textbooks were very popular, particularly *Lincoln's Botany* which was widely used in America and also translated into foreign languages for use in Europe. Mrs. Phelps supported the Greek, Hungarian, and Cuban movements for independence. However, she opposed the women's suffrage movement, and served as corresponding secretary of the Washington City Anti-Suffrage Society. Mrs. Phelps had high hopes that friendships among the students, who increasingly came from the South, and in the 1850s from the Deep South, would weaken regional

This fine school for girls opened in 1837 and operated until 1890; later it was used as a hotel, theater, nursing home, and private residence. The structure was then abandoned, vandalized, and eventually fell into ruin.

prejudices. She knew the girls would eventually become wives and mothers, and hoped they would influence their husbands and fathers to keep the Union together and save it from Civil War.

The Institute was popular from the very beginning of her tenure. Students came from Canada, the South, and even the Cherokee Nation. At the end of six months there were 62 pupils, including 40 boarders, eight resident teachers, and three assistant teachers. The school year consisted of two terms of 22 weeks each. Lodging, fuel, light, rent, and tuition cost $125 per term. There were extra charges for languages, music, and drawing lessons.

According to Ms. Mitchell, students were not permitted to visit Ellicotts Mills except under a teacher's supervision. Reading novels was strictly forbidden, and daily attendance at chapel compulsory. Students were expected to do the housekeeping in their own rooms, and served as monitors on a rotating basis, assisting the school administration in enforcing school rules. Ms. Mitchell wrote that in the winter the students were fond of eating maple syrup over snow. As a special treat, Almira Phelps sometimes hired a sleigh to take them riding over the snowy hills.

Mrs. Phelps left the school in 1856 after the death of her husband, and in 1891 the school finally closed, due to financial problems. The building went through various uses; it became a summer hotel known as Berg Alynwick, a private home, an early summer playhouse called Hilltop Theater, and a nursing home, before it was finally abandoned in the 1950s. The property is now owned by the county and will become an arboretum. The ruins of the Institute are now being stabilized as part of a public park.

Columbia Pike

In the late 1700s the pike was originally the road to Sandy Spring; much later it became Maryland Route 29. The first mention of this area was made by Martha Ellicott Tyson in her book, *Settlement of Ellicott's Mills.* She wrote that an oil mill and a carding mill for wool were built in 1804 by Joseph Atkinson on property he leased near the intersection of the road to Sandy Spring and the Baltimore/Frederick Turnpike (Main Street). The mill was supplied with water from the Wild Cat Branch; old plats call the river the Oil Mill Seat. Probably nothing remains from these early mills. Today the Pike is an important link in the limited roadway network through the old town.

The old stone portion of Taylor Furniture Store is a mid-19th century structure owned by John Fahey.

Taylor Furniture Store buildings

The stone section of this stone and frame building on the corner was built in the 1860s. The frame portion was probably added later.

John Fahey, an early member of the Catholic Church, arrived in town about 1822 and leased this property from Samuel Ellicott. By 1860 Fahey and Isaac Anderson (at one time the sheriff) occupied the two buildings at the corner. In those days the Tiber River flowed freely, and a wooden bridge permitted traffic to cross from Main Street to the Columbia Turnpike. A fire in 1915 damaged the building but it was rebuilt. Malone's Tavern and Al Kirn's barber and bicycle shops were other tenants at this

The assorted buildings on the east side of Columbia Pike have seen many changes. Among these have been grocery stores, a Ford dealership, a soda bottling company, and a Greek restaurant. The mural on the brick wall is a well-known, local landmark.

corner. More recently, Planned Parenthood occupied an office on the second floor of the stone building; Firestone Tires was on the first floor.

Three-story stone cinder block building

This structure was built in the 1920s. It has housed Crook's Grocery Store, an Acme Grocery Store, and a Greek restaurant. The adjacent one-story building was once the showroom for the Parlett Ford dealership next door.

One-story building set back from street: Taylor's

Possibly the soda water factory that E. C. Eckert of the Howard House operated and a livery were here as early as 1887. The present building, enlarged by the Parletts in the 1940s, was used by Z. Taylor "Bud" Ridgley for his soft drink bottling operation. The building then became Parlett Ford, which was operated by brothers Frank, Ralph, and Harry. The dealership used a number of buildings for a small showroom, repair shop, and offices. In more recent times it held Bert Anderson's Antique Imports.

3719 Columbia Pike: Wessel's Florist

This shop was built or remodeled as part of the Ford dealership. The upper floor was used as an apartment for the company's mechanic and later for the town policeman, Russell Moxley. The lower floor was a showroom and office. Later the Parletts' business moved to U.S. Route 40.

3723 Columbia Pike: Private residence

The Ellicotts sold this property to John Day, who constructed the house before 1860. The front portion of the house was the original part; by 1887 there were two rear and side additions.

Warehouses

Large frame sheds on both sides of the Pike are warehouses today, but they were once used as livery stables. On the west side of the turnpike in 1887, a blacksmith pounded out the iron work needed in town. A carpenter worked on the second floor. In this century the Green Cross Garage, which sold and repaired Chevrolet automobiles, occupied the building that runs from the Pike through to Hamilton Street.

Tongue Row

In the 1840s the widow Ann Tonge (pronounced like tongue) had these three double stone houses built. At that time, each double stone house was

Tongue Row, built in 1840s by the widow Ann Tonge, as it looked in the 1930s. Note the closed shutters.

assessed at $500. Note the stone-cut granite sills and lintels. Today the houses serve as homes and shops, and as picturesque panoramas for many photographers and artists who often set up their easels here.

Passageways between the charming granite block buildings lead to the parking lot behind the post office. The lot was added when town leaders realized that additional parking was needed if shoppers were to patronize Main Street merchants. Charles Miller and Isaac Taylor provided the property behind the new post office for the lot. Miller owned the Chevrolet dealership and Taylor owned the appliance store and movie theater. Both businessmen were well aware of the necessity for more parking.

The 1799 Quaker Meeting House closed over 150 years ago. It later served as a public school, hospital, and private school.

Other sites of interest

As the old road wanders up the hill, there are a variety of eye-catching and interesting sights. Not recommended for pedestrians, this trip is best taken by car. Some small houses near the road have been demolished; larger homes further away from the road are private residences. Across from Tongue Row and overlooking the town stands the Quaker Meeting House, one of the oldest buildings in Ellicott City. It is a private home, not open to the public.

The simple rectangular structure was built in 1799 from local granite. The building housed the Elkridge Preparatory Meeting until the 1830s. The

Meeting was closed when most of the Quakers had moved to Baltimore which offered more business opportunities.

Elizabeth Ellicott, widow of George, had a tin roof put on the building to help preserve it. The building has been used as a public school, a private school, a hospital, and a private home. The interior has been altered many times, and additions have been made.

A Quaker cemetery is adjacent to the Meeting House. The Ellicott family plot is enclosed by a granite wall. The private cemetery, owned and maintained by a corporation of family members, is still used for burials.

The Kraft home was enlarged for the Higinbothom Funeral Home. Today it is the Slack Funeral Home, operated by John Slack.

The building housing the Slack Funeral Home, which has been enlarged, was the Kraft family property. Since the Krafts were the local meat suppliers, they did their butchering in the outbuildings on the property. Another interesting building is across from Slack's and up the hill to the south — Dr. Taylor's residence and offices. It was a school for young men between the 1860s and 1900s, and was known first as St. Clement's and later as Maupin's University School (MUS).

Two elderly Ellicott City residents recount a fascinating story about the old house. Mark Moxley and Richard Talbott both remembered how Will Talbott made alterations to the large house after he purchased the property. The structure was much larger than Talbott needed, so he had the entire house shifted onto a new foundation. The first floor of the building was removed and scrapped, leaving the smaller structure that stands today.

Thus ends our tour of historic Ellicott City. If you have any questions about the town or have additional information for the next volume, please contact the author, Joetta Cramm, in care of Greenberg Publishing Company at 7566 Main Street, Sykesville, Maryland 21784.

ABOUT THE AUTHOR

For over 15 years, Joetta Cramm has been teaching local history through Howard Community College's credit-free program. Joetta supplemented this very successful course with tours of Ellicott City and the county. In addition, she has researched, and continues to research, local properties to provide documented records of individual properties.

Joetta Cramm moved to Maryland in 1961 after graduating from Western Illinois University and having taught in Illinois and South Dakota. She raised her family in Ellicott City and was active in community activities. In the early 1960s, she enjoyed taking her young sons to the B&O Railroad Station to see the passing trains as they rumbled by. From talking with Main Street's barbers, the Cavey brothers, while her sons were getting haircuts, Joetta became intrigued with local events and people.

As President of the American Association of University Women, Joetta worked with its members to develop a walking tour of Ellicott City for the town's 1972 Bicentennial activities. Later, she worked as a legistlative assistant for ten years with the Howard County Council. Currently she is President of the Howard County Tourism Council, and continues to teach Howard County history. Joetta enjoys speaking about the history of Ellicott City and Howard County, and always welcomes questions or new information about Ellicott City.

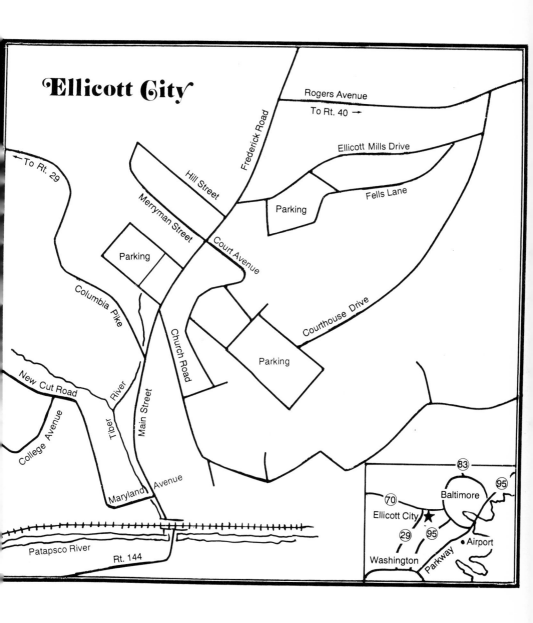

Ellicott City